Cultivate

Cultivate

How God Grows the Fruit of the Spirit within Us

Richard Kannwischer

Cultivate: How God Grows the Fruit of the Spirit within Us

Published by Forefront Books, Nashville, Tennessee.
Distributed by Simon & Schuster.

Library of Congress Control Number: 2025921396

Print ISBN: 978-1-63763-530-8
E-book ISBN: 978-1-63763-531-5

Cover Design by ArtSpeak Creative
Interior Design by PerfecType, Nashville, TN.

Printed in the United States of America

26 27 28 29 30 31 RR4 10 9 8 7 6 5 4 3 2 1

To Danica and Ashby—
May your roots go down deep into the love of God,
and may your lives always bear fruit
that blesses the world and glorifies the One who planted you.
Thank you for the honor of being called your father.

CONTENTS

FOREWORD

God has built grace into your brain in the form of neuroplasticity.

Have you ever considered this? The maker of the universe designed your mind with the possibility of change. This physiological fact reflects a deeper spiritual one: we were made to grow.

Grace is not theoretical. It is the reality of both spiritual and physical life.

This means you are not stuck—not with the mental health you have now, the addictions you battle, or the fears you carry. God made you to change.

In that sense, we really are like soil. We were made to be cultivated and produce fruit.

Cultivation is the central premise of the book you are about to read. It is also one of the central premises of the Bible. Jesus constantly spoke in parables of farming, because he knew that humans were made to be cultivated. Paul picks up the same metaphor when he writes what has now become one of the most famous Bible passages in history: the fruit of the Spirit.

There are a few reasons I love the way the book you're about to read approaches this topic.

First, because Richard tells so many stories. Not only are stories so enjoyable to read, but they bring real life to the abstract. Stories are testimonies, reminding us that God actually changes his people.

Second, Richard's writing reminds me that the fruit of the Spirit are the good life. We often mistake virtue for a burden rather than a gift. But every page of this book reminds me that becoming more loving, more patient, more kind *means becoming more like Jesus*! And that, of course, is where our deepest happiness lies. I've heard it said that obedience is not how we earn our salvation, but it is often how we enjoy it. Consider this book a roadmap, then, to enjoying the good life that God is calling you to.

Finally, as the title suggests, I love how clear Richard is about how change works. It's slow, grace-based, and comes from looking at Jesus. "Look at the captain!" (This will make more sense after you read Chapter 3.) Books on how to live can often be fraught with the burden of "quick fixes" and a "just do this" mentality. That's the opposite of the biblical path of change that Richard shows here. It's rooted in what God does for us, and slow as a garden—but just as real.

This book will leave you not only full of ideas on how to cultivate the fruit of the Spirit in your life, but it will also leave your gaze on Jesus, so that we might become what we behold.

Justin Whitmel Earley
Business lawyer and author of *Habits of the Household*, *The Body Teaches the Soul*, and others
Richmond, 2025

PREFACE

HOW TO GET THE MOST FROM THIS BOOK

Very truly I tell you, unless a kernel of wheat falls to the ground and dies, it remains only a single seed. But if it dies, it produces many seeds.

—John 12:24

I didn't think much of the meeting at the time.

He had questions—about God, about prayer, and about heaven. I'd had hundreds of conversations like that before. As a pastor, I was used to them. Trained for them. Comfortable with them.

I listened, nodded, answered as best I could. We ended our time praying together, and then I walked him to the door and moved on to the next meeting of the day.

The following morning, I saw his face in the news.

The man who had sat in my office the day before had gone home, murdered his wife and son, and then thrown himself in front of a train.

I came undone.

Not all at once. But over the days that followed, something in me collapsed. I kept replaying the conversation in my head. *What did I miss? Why didn't I see it?* I felt like a failure. And worse, like I wasn't fit for ministry at all.

By what I can only describe as providence, I had already committed to attend a two-week doctoral seminar at a monastery led by the philosopher and Christian author Dallas Willard. I had read his books and deeply admired his mind. I went expecting good classes and good content. Instead, I found something much deeper.

Dallas pulled up in an old car, looking every bit the part of a weathered and seasoned professor. But there was something startlingly alive about him too. He was one of the smartest people I've ever met but also one of the humblest. He was strong but not domineering. He listened to you as if you were the most important person in the world and as if he had all the time in the world.

He didn't rush. He didn't preach. He simply lived each moment in God's goodness. And in my pain, he invited me to rediscover God's goodness alongside him. He had compassion on me. He listened to me. He prayed for me.

Dallas didn't give me techniques. He gave me vision. He reminded me that the goal of the Christian life isn't just to answer people's questions more effectively. It's to become a different kind of person from the inside out.

Because you can look composed on the outside and still be unraveling within. You can say all the right things and still live without peace, without joy, and without change. And that doesn't just apply to the man who came to see me. It applies to me. And to you.

That season broke something in me. But it also became the breaking ground for God to work in me.

Jesus once said, "Unless a kernel of wheat falls to the ground and dies, it remains only a single seed. But if it dies, it produces many seeds" (John 12:24). I hadn't realized it at the time, but that moment of my collapse was also the beginning of my cultivation. God was tilling the soil of my life. And from that moment on, I knew I didn't want to spend my life simply running church programs or delivering polished sermons. I wanted to help people be transformed by grace. I wanted to become the kind of person who is truly shaped by God's Spirit.

When I came home from that retreat, my wife took one look at me at the airport and said, "What happened? You look . . . different."

And as heavy as that season was, I want you to hear this:

Real change is possible. Even in the harshest seasons.

That is true for all of us. And that is what I am inviting you to participate in as you read and interact with this book.

A Wild Ride

One of the most joyful, faith-filled people you could ever meet is a man named Dan Adragna. He attends Twin Lakes Church in Santa Cruz, where my friend René Schlaepfer pastors the congregation. (René and I go way back. We were pastors together in California. You should pray for him, though. He's served in Santa Cruz for decades. That kind of beauty can soften a preacher. It's why my family moved to Atlanta from a similar paradise—Newport Beach was just too much. We didn't want heaven to be a letdown. But back to Dan.)

Dan had already been through a storm—divorce, disillusionment, years of spiritual dryness. But in that ache, grace found him. His faith came alive. His joy became contagious. You couldn't be around Dan without feeling the goodness of God radiating from him.

Then came the ultimate test.

One Christmas Eve, Dan couldn't shake a cough. His daughter urged him to go get checked. He drove himself to the ER, collapsed in the waiting room, and wouldn't wake up for two months.

He had contracted a rare viral pneumonia, which quickly became life-threatening. He coded three times. An infection developed. Gangrene spread. The doctors did all they could, but he lost both legs, most of his fingers, part of his nose and ears, even a portion of his skull. The tracheal tube damaged his vocal cords.

When he finally regained consciousness, he looked down and discovered he had no legs.

When René rushed into his hospital room, Dan turned to him with a crooked grin and rasped, "Pastor, I woke up and discovered I'm not half the man I used to be."

Wait, what?

Dan wasn't being flippant. He wasn't living in denial. But neither had he lost his sense of humor in that coma. His joy—real joy—was still there, still shining.

He had every reason to curse the heavens. But instead, Dan clung to a deeper truth: that his broken body would one day be made whole. That Jesus is the firstborn from the dead—and the foretaste of a new creation dawning. That everything sad will come untrue, and it will somehow be greater than we could possibly imagine. That Christian hope would become the seedbed for his laughter, even in the loss.

Later, Dan talked about riding "Invertigo," one of those hanging track roller coasters at Six Flags. (If you want to see what I'm talking about, stop reading and check out a YouTube video for full effect.) A fourth-grade girl was seated directly across from him, and their legs were dangling in the air as they faced each other. As the ride progressed, Dan's prosthetic legs loosened through the loops and barrel rolls. Then they began to lift at a biologically impossible angle before they started twisting like pinwheels in a stiff breeze. And then they flew away.

One leg. Then the other.

Torpedo one—go!
Torpedo two—go!

The girl screamed. Dan tried to explain, but he couldn't get the words out.

"I tried," he said, "but I was laughing too hard."

That's who Dan is.

Dan now joyfully partakes in the work of the kingdom by partnering with Joni & Friends and other organizations, helping people with disabilities find purpose, dignity, and hope.

Not despite what he's lost, but because of what he's found.

Have you found it?

I want to be more like Dan. He is a living reminder that the Spirit really can cultivate joy in suffering, peace in pain, and goodness in broken soil. He shows us that even when life strips away what we once relied on, we are not beyond hope. God can grow something beautiful right where everything felt broken.

I know the gospel begins with the awareness God already loves me as I am, but I'm also sure I was never meant to stay this way. I am still too petty, too grumpy, too anxious, too quick-tempered, too critical . . . and the list could go on.

Loosening Hard Ground

It's strange how often new life starts in hard ground. Sometimes it's a hospital bed. Sometimes it's heartbreak or failure or collapse.

But again and again, I've seen and experienced grace in the very place I thought would be barren. And when you encounter it enough times, you start to ask different questions. *How do I fix my situation?* becomes *What might God be growing here?*

The goal of the Christian life is not perfect circumstances where everything is easy. God's aim is for us to become a particular kind of people, marked in a distinct way.

That's what this book is about.

I've been a pastor for over a quarter of a century, and much of this project comes out of the holy restlessness of complacency in our character development. My experience tells me that people want to grow but don't know how. Church leaders have confused religious activity with spiritual maturity.

I have spent way too much time running a Christian organization and not near enough effort equipping individuals and families to develop into more flourishing people.

The Christian life is not merely attending worship services and volunteering to help the less fortunate. A friend of mine says we need to be careful that church doesn't become a Rotary Club with better music.

To be clear, I think gathering to worship is crucial to your regular rhythms. And it is impossible to follow Jesus without being generous to others with your time and resources. I am also a member of Rotary International, so I'm on board with making our communities stronger through service.

What gets lost in all of this is the question, *Who am I becoming?* Am I substantively any different in character than I was a year ago? I have been rescued by God, but to what end? The rest of my days can't be simply a holding pattern for the sweet relief of forgiveness and the promises of life after death.

The Bible says there is more to the work of God than mercy and eternal rest. We were made to bear fruit that will last.

The apostle Paul calls this work "the fruit of the Spirit"—love, joy, peace, patience, kindness, goodness, faithfulness, gentleness, and self-control—which can actually grow in the messy, complicated soil of your real life.

This book is called *Cultivate* because that's exactly what the Spirit of God does: God is a gardener who cultivates something in us that we could never grow on our own. He doesn't ask us to fake it or force it. He invites us to be rooted in him—to let him do his work in us.

If you've ever felt stuck, jaded, overwhelmed, or tired of trying to change yourself, you're not alone. And you're not without help. God's presence is already at work in you, breaking ground in places you thought were lifeless. If you'll let him, he will grow something in you that lasts.

My prayer is that by the time you reach the final page, you'll not only see and understand the fruit of the Spirit more clearly, but you'll also want to join him in the slow, sacred work of cultivation in your own life.

How to Use This Book

This book isn't meant to just motivate you. It's meant to be a companion on your journey. And so you will find that you will be invited to do more than merely read each chapter.

Each chapter begins by helping you see the character of God more clearly, because you can't bear fruit until you're connected to the source. Then we'll look at how that aspect of the Spirit's life shows up in the real world—in your conversations, your habits, your pressures, your relationships.

At the close of each chapter after the introduction, you'll find an interactive section titled "An Invitation for Reflection & Growth." Each of these sections contains three parts: a few guiding scriptures, along with reflection questions and exercises; a cultivating practice that will help each aspect of fruit take root in your life; and a closing prayer for you to pray repeatedly to deepen God's work of cultivation in you.

The interactive sections can be done by yourself or as part of a group. They aren't assignments; instead, they're invitations. Think of them as gentle handholds for your spiritual journey, small tools for soul-tending, designed to help the words you've read travel from your head to your heart, and from your heart into your everyday life. And don't rush through them. The invitation is to linger and return. Pray more than once. Ask the Spirit to show you where he's already at work in the garden of your life.

This book isn't just for information and inspiration. My prayer is that within these pages, you will begin to experience true transformation through the work of Christ.

Let's get started.

INTRODUCTION

LEARNING TO TEND

I still remember the first time I was asked to cultivate something.

It was in a high school science class. Our teacher, Mr. Knipper, had convinced the administration to let him build a small garden on the edge of campus, right up against the fence where the sun beat down and the soil was more rock than earth. Most of us weren't exactly thrilled. We'd signed up for *science*, not thinking that meant dirt under our fingernails in the Texas heat. But the assignment was clear: We had to plant, water, weed, and tend our little plot week after week.

I'd never worked so hard for a vegetable in my life.

My hometown in Central Texas isn't known for easy ground. The soil is stubborn. The sun is relentless. But slowly, something was happening. Green shoots pushed through the dust. Tiny blooms opened into vegetables. And one day, I pulled a carrot from the ground that I had planted myself. It was crooked. It was ugly. Dirt clung to it. But I swear, it was the best carrot I had ever eaten.

Not because it tasted sweeter or juicier than others I'd had, but because I had cared for it. I had waited on it. I had worked for it, and I had helped cultivate it.

That little garden taught me something school alone never did: Growth is amazing, but it is not automatic. This is exactly what I don't want you to miss about God. He not only made you, but he is also tending to you. You are his Adam, his earth. And he is actively working the soil of your life.

The One Who Cultivates

Before anything else, God is a gardener.

Yes, he is the Creator—the Maker of all things—but Scripture introduces him with earthy specificity. He doesn't begin with blueprints or battle cries. His first act is planting: "Now the Lord God had planted a garden" (Genesis 2:8).

His words are seeds:

> "Let there be light."
> "Let the land produce vegetation."

He bends down, shapes humanity from dust, and breathes his own Spirit into our lungs.

Before God gives laws, he plants. Before he gives instruction, he gives life. Before he calls us to worship, he is shaping us.

If we want to understand who God is—and who we are—this is where we begin. We were made in the image of the One who cultivates. The word *adam* in Hebrew literally means "ground."

See this: We weren't made just to believe or behave—we were made to be planted and flourish. You were made from the dust of earth and planted here to flourish for God's kingdom.

Something in you was always meant to grow.

Why Cultivate?

Most of us don't wake up to roosters or spend afternoons coaxing tomatoes out of reluctant soil. We live in suburbs and cities, cradle laptops more than shovels, and scroll through feeds instead of walking fence lines. So, before we press on, let's name the obvious:

You can love this book and still be terrible with houseplants.

To cultivate means more than to dig or plant. The Latin root *colere* means "to till," but it also means "to cherish," "to honor," and "to care for." We use it every day without thinking.

We cultivate a skill—through repeated practice, until it reshapes us.
We cultivate a friendship—through time, presence, and shared burdens.
We cultivate an environment—through habits, rhythms, and values.

In all these things, something raw is shaped into something rich. Intention replaces impulse. Care replaces neglect. Cultivating is the opposite of drifting.

That's what makes this metaphor so essential to the Christian life.

Because God isn't just interested in what you know or what you've done. He's interested in who you are becoming. He's not content with cosmetic change; he wants character that runs deep.

The common thread? Intentional growth. Something *raw and unformed* is tended toward something *rich and fruitful.*

That is precisely the Spirit's work in a life: hidden, patient, persistent, turning rocky places into good ground.

But let's also not be naïve: God is not the only one eager to shape you. Whether you realize it or not, something is always forming you, nudging your desires, shaping your habits, steering your affections. These influences don't usually show up with warning labels. They slip in through screens, conversations, headlines, and routines. Take the almighty algorithm, for example. It learns what your eyes linger on, what you scroll past, and what you click. And then, quietly and relentlessly, it feeds you more of the same, curating your view of the world and training your heart in ways that are almost invisible.

Advertising works the same way. It doesn't just sell you products; it sells you a story: *You're not enough, but this will help.* It plants a seed of discontent, then offers the fix. The workplace has its own shaping power too. Productivity becomes a proxy for worth. Titles and performance reviews quietly whisper that you are what you earn. LinkedIn becomes a drug for overachievers. And it's not just screens or systems; it's people. Friends, coworkers, online voices—all of them carry influence. Peer pressure doesn't end in high school; it just gets more sophisticated. Without even realizing it, we start to imitate the rhythms and values of those around us.

You are always being cultivated by something. The real question is, *Who's holding the shovel?*

This book invites you to place the care of your soul back into the true Gardener's hands—to trust his rhythms over a culture of hurry, his pruning over social media's pull, his harvest over the world's hype.

Whether you live on acreage or in a city where a garden isn't in sight, keep the word *cultivate* close. Let it remind you that God's Spirit is already at work beneath the surface, turning ordinary days into fertile ground. Your task is to stay open, rooted, and ready for the growth only he can give.

Fruit, Thorns, and Vines

In the beginning, God's first blessing to humanity was simple and clear: "Be fruitful" (Genesis 1:28).

God's blessing carries a calling: to bring forth life, to reflect his image, and to multiply good.

But something went wrong.

Though the soil was good and the purpose clear, Adam and Eve turned from the voice that formed them. They grasped for control and, in doing so, broke something deep. Not just in their relationship with God, but in the very ground beneath them.

Work became toil. Fruitfulness became frustration. Thorns and thistles grew.

And still, God never revoked the calling.

The ache we feel when life resists growth—that longing for more—isn't weakness. It's memory. It's a soul-deep recognition that things were meant to be different. You were made for more than survival. You were made to walk with God and help cultivate with him.

That's why Jesus comes not just as teacher but as vine: "I am the true vine, and my Father is the gardener. . . . If you remain in me and I in you, you will bear much fruit" (John 15:1, 5).

Jesus doesn't simply rescue us, he reconnects us. The story of cultivation isn't lost, it's restored. And the Spirit he gives is still at work, right now, in the soil of your everyday life.

Being Cultivated

I experienced this deep cultivation not just in theory, but through a man I barely knew when I was twenty-one years old.

It started with a meeting. I was in college, tasked with asking a university trustee—an imposing, sharply dressed investment banker—for a donation to support our music program. I expected a polite nod, maybe a delayed response. Instead, he didn't hesitate. He wrote a check on the spot. But then he looked me in the eye and asked a question I didn't know how to answer.

"How well do you want to know me?"

I blinked. I was confused. It didn't seem like the kind of question a busy man with a Wall Street résumé would ask a college kid. I stumbled out something like, "Sure, I want to know you."

He nodded, almost solemnly. And then he started to talk.

He didn't talk about his business or the university. He told me his story. He opened up about his own life, sharing the good and, more surprisingly, the struggle. He was transparent in a way that made me uncomfortable. Vulnerable in a way I didn't know how to respond to. And then he said something that completely unsettled me.

"I know that God loves me through it all, despite all I've done. And I know who I'm becoming. The question is, do you know that about you?"

I didn't. Not really.

That conversation turned into many. We met repeatedly over the years. He asked questions no one else asked. Penetrating questions. Difficult questions. Soul questions. And slowly, I trusted him enough to tell the truth. Nothing held back. We read Scripture, not to dissect it, but to apply it. To let it do its work in us.

At the time, I didn't know what to call it. I just knew I was being seen, challenged, loved. But now I know the term: I had a spiritual director. And I entrusted him with the care of my soul.

It doesn't have to be a formal title or relationship, but it is an intentional process, and it's more than a little scary.

I was being cultivated into someone new.

Because that's what cultivation is: not just something God does *to* you, but something God does *with* you. Slowly. Patiently. Personally. He tends the places in your life that feel hidden or hardened.

He waters what looks barren. He pulls up what chokes the roots. And over time, sometimes without you even realizing it, something begins to grow.

That's the work we're stepping into together.

This book isn't a set of instructions to follow or a checklist to complete. It's more like a walk through the garden of your life—sometimes quiet, sometimes surprising, sometimes uncomfortable. In each chapter, we'll pause and pay attention to what God is doing beneath the surface. I'll help you listen for his voice, notice what's growing, and name the things that need to be cleared away.

You don't have to know everything. You might not feel ready. What God asks at the beginning is for us to be willing.

So what will all of this look like? What will begin to take shape when the Spirit of God tends the soil of your soul?

Paul called it *fruit*.

And that's where we're headed next.

THE FRUIT OF THE SPIRIT

We live in an age of accelerated outrage.

Scroll the headlines, and you'll see it everywhere: tempers flaring at school board meetings, road rage exploding on highways, viral videos of passengers losing it on planes, and political debates that feel more like cage matches than conversations. You see it in workplaces, on social media, even in churches. People interrupt, accuse, attack, withdraw. And more and more, we're starting to expect it.

We brace for defensiveness. We assume bad intentions. We roll our eyes, shake our heads, and whisper things like, "It is what it is." Impatience has become a badge of pride. Kindness is dismissed as weakness. Self-control feels optional. And love—the real kind, the steady, sacrificial, enemy-embracing kind—can feel like a fairy tale from another time.

In a world like this, it's easy to become cynical. It's easy to assume this is just how life works. But something deep inside us knows better. We long for a different way of being. Not just behavior tweaks, but real renovation.

Is there another way to live?

The apostle Paul believed there was, and *not just a better strategy, but a better source.*

He wrote a letter to a group of early Christians in a place called Galatia, a region where spiritual confusion and cultural pressure were pulling people in opposite directions. Some were trying to earn their worth by strict religious rule-keeping. Others were chasing freedom that had no center or guardrails. One group was motivated by fear, the other by appetite. But the result was the same: frustration, division, and soul-level exhaustion.

Paul called it life "in the flesh." And he knew it well. He had lived it, both as a religious zealot and a man shaped by power and performance.

But Paul had been transformed. And in his letter to the Galatians, he paints a vivid contrast between two ways of being: the self-guided life and the Spirit-led life. One produces competition, chaos, and control. The other cultivates something much deeper: *a life that reflects the character of Christ.*

And to describe that life, Paul doesn't reach for a list of rules or accomplishments. He reaches for a garden.

Because when the Spirit of God is at work in someone, something begins to grow.

Not artificially. Not instantly. But organically, like fruit slowly ripening over time.

The Drift of the Flesh

You can't grow the fruit of the Spirit in the soil of selfishness.

Before Paul sketches a radiant orchard, he issues a sober warning. In Galatians 5:13–21, he opens the gate to a different field, the one we drift into when no one is watching the soil.

Picture an abandoned garden. No malicious act was required to ruin it; all it took was neglect. Weeds sprout first—small jealousies, whispered comparisons. Soon thistles of anger crowd out tenderness, their barbs catching every passerby. Bitterness spreads like bindweed, wrapping tight around joy until sunlight can't get in. Leave it longer and rot sets in: unchecked appetites, fractured friendships, distorted selves.

Paul names the fruit of that neglect in blunt strokes—sexual misconduct, manipulative spirituality, rivalry that turns conversations into cage fights, nights that blur into hangovers, a life ruled by impulse instead of love.

It's a vivid reminder: If the Spirit isn't sowing, the flesh is.

That's why self-improvement alone can't save us. We need the right gardener. We need a different seed. And that is exactly what Paul describes next: "But the fruit of the Spirit is love, joy, peace, [patience], kindness, goodness, faithfulness, gentleness and self-control" (Galatians 5:22–23—please note that the New International Version uses a more archaic word, *forbearance*, instead of the much more useful word *patience* in the list. The New Revised Standard Version, updated edition, agrees with me. So in this book you will encounter *patience*.).

The Gift of the Spirit

Notice a few things.

First, it's God's fruit. Not yours. Not a task list. Not a badge of earning. It comes from abiding in the Spirit, not from greater willpower. This fruit isn't an indication of a particular personality profile. It's a harvest.

Second, the word is *fruit*. Notice that it's singular. Not *fruits*. Paul isn't offering a menu of spiritual traits. He's describing one unified life, rooted in the Spirit, producing a singular, beautiful result.

Third, this fruit comes with context. Galatians 5:13–26 is all about freedom—not the freedom to do anything, but the freedom to become who you were made to be. Paul contrasts the acts of the flesh with the fruit of the Spirit. One path is corrosive. The other is rooted, resilient, and life-giving.

This is one of the central convictions of this book: A life led by the Spirit of God bears the kind of fruit the world longs for and you were created for.

It's easy to mistake activity for growth, to think spiritual maturity means going to more programs or volunteering or reading more devotionals. But real evidence of a life rooted in God isn't attendance or activity. It's love. Joy. Peace. Patience. Kindness. Goodness. Faithfulness. Gentleness. Self-control. This is the target, the goal, the aim.

Look at the list again with truth serum in your veins. Is that who you are becoming?

What This Book Is—and Isn't

This book is not a how-to manual. It's not a self-help guide dressed in spiritual language. It's not a list of virtues for you to try harder to master.

It's a journey of lasting and eternal change.

Each chapter ahead explores a distinct aspect of the fruit of the Spirit—signs of true life, grown by the Spirit and shaped by God.

That's why each chapter begins with what God does:

- **Love**—*The One Who Won't Let Go*
  Not niceness, not tolerance, but a self-giving, enemy-embracing, cross-shaped love.

- **Joy**—*The One Who Gives You a Song*
  A joy not dependent on outcomes but anchored in presence, even in sorrow.

- **Peace**—*The One Who Calms the Storm*
  Not escape from trouble but calm within it, a heart settled in God.

- **Patience**—*The One Who Waits with You*
  Endurance without resentment. A holy slowness in a culture of hurry.

- **Kindness**—*The One Who Pours Out*
  Not random acts, but intentional mercy that heals.

- **Goodness**—*The One Who Mends What's Broken*
  Moral clarity with compassion. Integrity that shines in the darkness.

- **Faithfulness**—*The One Who Keeps His Promises*
  A long obedience. Steadiness. Loyalty to God and others, even when it's hard.

- **Gentleness**—*The One Who Speaks Tenderly*
  Strength restrained by love. Courage without cruelty.

- **Self-Control**—*The One Who Trains You*
  Not self-suppression, but Spirit-empowered mastery of desire and direction.

Because before any of this fruit shows up through you, it begins in him. This is God's work. You are not the gardener; you are the ground. This does not mean you have no role to play. But you do need to remember that this is a partnership.

Where to Begin

Paul gives us a kind of pattern for how cultivation works. After describing the fruit of the Spirit, he writes, "Those who *belong to Christ Jesus* have *crucified the flesh* with its passions and desires. Since we live by the Spirit, let us *keep in step with the Spirit*" (Galatians 5:24–25, emphasis mine).

There's a sacred rhythm to this life—three movements that begin to shape us into people who bear fruit that lasts:

Movement #1: Belong to Christ

It all begins not with guilt, but with a gift. That's where the roots go deepest.

There's a moment in *Toy Story 2* that captures this perfectly. Woody, the cowboy doll, gets stolen by a toy collector who wants to sell him to a museum. Woody is cleaned up, polished, and restored, but something's missing. Over time, Woody begins to forget who he really is. Then one day, he sees an old TV commercial where a boy embraces a toy just like him and it clicks. He rubs off the fresh paint on the bottom of his boot and sees the name "Andy" scrawled in ink. That's all it takes. Woody now remembers where he belongs.

We forget too. Somewhere along the way, we stop hearing the voice of the One who made us. But you haven't been forgotten, and you haven't been left to figure this out alone. The One who formed you still cares what and who you become.

And maybe that's the most important thing for you to remember right now: You belong to Jesus Christ. His name is already written on you.

Movement #2: Crucify Destructive Desires

Of course, growth also means letting go. And this is where it gets painful.

Most of us are a little too comfortable with our brokenness. We don't love it, but we've made peace with it. We try to manage our sin rather than kill it. But the goal of cultivation isn't maintenance; it's transformation.

C. S. Lewis offers a searing image of this in *The Great Divorce*. A man journeys from hell toward heaven with a small red lizard on his shoulder. The lizard is constantly whispering poisonous lies in his ear. An angel approaches and offers to silence the creature and free the man from its influence, which the man thinks he wants.

> "Then I will kill it," the angel says.
> "Oh—look out! You're burning me," the man protests.
> "Keep away."
> "Don't you want him killed?"
> "You didn't say anything about killing him . . ."

Excuse after excuse, the man backpedals from the freedom he claims to want.

Lewis's point is devastatingly clear: Sometimes we prefer the hell we know to the heaven we don't. We can become disturbingly comfortable with our own dysfunction and destruction.

Is there a habit, desire, or addiction you've been hiding or harboring? Something you've just learned to live with? You don't have to keep feeding what's devastating you. You can surrender it. Right now. The Spirit of the living God is ready to help—not just to silence the lies, but to set you free.

Movement #3: Keep in Step with the Spirit

Now for a lighter confession. During my sophomore year of college in San Antonio, I needed a P.E. credit. I had played a lot of sports growing up, but I wanted to try something new. So, when a pretty girl invited me to take Couples Country & Western Dancing with her and some friends, I signed up.

One afternoon, someone on the varsity dance team (the "Ropers") got sick. They needed a fill-in or the whole routine would be scrapped. I had seen the routine once or twice, but I'd never danced it. I was nowhere near ready.

Then Amy, one of the best dancers in the group, turned to me and said, "Come on, Rich. Trust me. Just follow me. I know the routine. All you've got to do is keep in step. No matter what, 1-2-3, 2-2-3. You can do it." (That's a waltz, by the way.)

I was terrified. I had no idea what I was doing except for the basics. But I followed, and while it wasn't perfect, it was still beautiful.

Not because I was impressive, but because of the one I was dancing with.

You may feel like I did that day, like you're faking it, stumbling through, unsure how to move forward. But if you'll keep in step with the Spirit—even if you don't fully know the routine—it can still be beautiful.

That's what this journey is about: learning to listen for the rhythm of God's Spirit, following his lead, and allowing the fruit of his presence to grow over time.

You were made for more than image management. You were made to walk with God.

And that walk begins here, with one step. One step away from the self-absorption of the age. One step away from the performance trap. One step away from self-improvement projects and toward spiritual surrender. One step away from the thorns of anger, envy, and impulse, and into the soil of grace and renewal.

Trying harder alone won't get you to where you are called to be. You can't manufacture fruit. You don't need to fix yourself before God begins his work. That's the beauty of the gospel: God is already tending the soil. He is already planting seeds.

All you're asked to do is stay rooted. Stay available and keep in step.

The Spirit is already at work—quietly, faithfully—shaping you into the kind of person who bears life for the world.

So, as you turn the page, allow these chapters to challenge you, stretch you, guide you. Let them lead you into deeper trust and a closer walk.

Because this isn't just a book. It's an invitation.

You were made to flourish, to bear this kind of fruit. And the journey starts now, with one faithful, Spirit-led step in love.

An Invitation for Reflection & Growth

KEY VERSE

The fruit of the righteous is a tree of life,
and the one who is wise saves lives.
—Proverbs 11:30

BIG IDEA

We were made to cultivate. But sin damages the soil of our lives, eroding purpose, wounding relationships, and distorting our work. Still, God has not abandoned his garden. In Christ, he is tending, pruning, and restoring us so we can bear fruit again. Not just any fruit, but fruit that nourishes others and echoes into eternity.

READING & REFLECTION

What You Were Made For

Read Genesis 1:26–31; 2:15–17; 3:17–19

- What does it mean to "bear fruit" in the context of creation as described in Genesis?
- How do you see the original calling to cultivate—relationally, vocationally, spiritually—playing out in your life today?
- In what ways has sin distorted your sense of calling, purpose, or work?

Reflection & Practice

- Name one area where fruitfulness feels more like futility. Ask God to show you what restoration might look like there.

When Fear Takes Root

Read Numbers 13:17–33

- What fears keep you from stepping into the life God is calling you to cultivate?
- How does fear, like it did for the Israelite spies, distort your perception of reality?
- What's one "next faithful step" you've been avoiding?

Reflection & Practice

- Are there parts of your life you have hidden out of fear?
- Are there "red lizards" on your shoulder? Perhaps these are voices, habits, or wounds you need the courage to release to move forward. What might it look like to release them and move forward in faith?

God as Gardener

Read John 15:1–8

- What does it mean to abide in Christ?
- How is abiding different from striving or doing more?
- What spiritual rhythms help you stay connected to the Vine?

Reflection & Practice

- Where might you need to prune? Name one area that's consuming your energy but not bearing fruit, then consider how God might be inviting you to let it go.

The War Within

Read Galatians 5:13–26 and Proverbs 11:30

- Where do you feel the tension between the Spirit and the flesh in your daily life?
- How can you begin cultivating your inner life so that the Spirit has room to grow fruit?
- Which fruit of the Spirit feels most needed—and most lacking—in this season?

Reflection & Practice

- Each morning for a week, slowly read Galatians 5:22–23. Choose one fruit to reflect on and pray over each day.

CULTIVATION PRACTICE: START WITH THE SOIL

In a journal, draw a circle and divide it into three areas:

Character—Who you're becoming
Relationships—Who you're walking with
Purpose—What you're tending

In each section, write:

- One place where you see signs of growth
- One area that feels dry, crowded, or in need of care

Let this reflection serve as a kind of spiritual "soil sample"—an honest snapshot of where you are on the journey. Then spend time in prayer, asking the Spirit to tend the struggling places and cultivate fruit where roots are taking hold.

Growth doesn't always look dramatic. But even naming what's happening underground is a faithful act of cultivation.

A PRAYER TO CULTIVATE FRUIT OF THE SPIRIT

Lord Jesus,
thank you that I belong to you—
not because I have earned it,
but because you have claimed me as your own.
Your name is written over my life,
and nothing can take me from your hand.

Father,
you know the desires in me that distort your image.
Give me courage to release what pulls me away from you—
habits that harm, loves that enslave,
attitudes that do not reflect your grace.
By your Spirit, put to death what is destructive,
and set me free to live in your goodness.

Holy Spirit,
teach me your rhythm.
Help me listen for your voice,
follow your lead,
and move at your pace.
Form in me your love, your joy, your peace—
and every quality that is true of you—
so that my life bears the beauty of your character
in a world longing for what only you can give.

Amen.

CHAPTER ONE

LOVE

The One Who Won't Let Go

I was a sophomore in high school when my friend's dad—one of the most respected adults in our church—volunteered to lead our Sunday school class. For three months, he was our teacher, and to this day it remains one of the most thoughtful, engaging, and earnest learning experiences I've ever been part of.

He gave us just one question: *What is love?*

That was it. The same question. Every week.

We debated. We read Scripture. We looked at philosophers like Aristotle: *To love is to will the good of the other.* We talked about infatuation, friendship, marriage, sacrifice, and we pushed one another.

By the end of our time together, we were required to come up with our own working definition of *love*.

After weeks of wrestling, we landed on this: *Love is an unconditional commitment that enables full human potential.*

We were proud of that definition. It sounded weighty and serious and even a little noble. I still remember the sense of accomplishment when we wrote it out on the easel that final week. It felt like we had done something important.

And then, not long after the class ended, my friend stopped coming to church.

I found out weeks later that his father—the man who had guided our entire study on love—had been having an affair with the youth director the entire time he was teaching us.

I was shocked.

It felt like the whole thing had collapsed under its own weight. The very person who led us in defining love had somehow betrayed it in the process.

And that's when I realized something I've never forgotten:

There is a difference between being able to define love and being defined by love.
There is a difference between discussing love and dwelling in it.
There is a difference between saying what love is and becoming the kind of person through whom love lives.

We begin this journey through the fruit of the Spirit where Paul begins: with love. Not as a concept to admire or a virtue to chase, but as something far deeper—more lived than defined, more embodied than explained.

If we want love to take root, we'll need more than a classroom conversation and definition.

Counterfeit Love

Before we can grasp what love truly is, we need to be clear about what it is not. In a world flooded with counterfeits and confusion, it's easy to settle for a cheap imitation.

Not everything that claims the name of love deserves it.

We've grown jaded, worn down by fractured marriages, hollow vows, and empty promises. The world can feel so heavy that at times we begin to doubt whether real love is even possible.

Years ago, when I moved from Texas to New Jersey, I was homesick and culture-shocked. One day, while navigating the chaos that is Route 1, I spotted a sign that felt like a message from heaven: "Genuine Tex-Mex Cuisine." My stomach and soul both rejoiced. I pulled in, ordered green chicken enchiladas—the gold standard of any true Tex-Mex restaurant—and took two hopeful bites.

That was all I could manage.

It wasn't genuine. It was a cheap imitation.

That's what Paul is getting at when he writes to the church in Rome, "Let love be genuine" (Romans 12:9 NRSVue).

The Greek word Paul uses—*anupokritos*—literally means "unhypocritical." In other words, no pretending. No performance. No plating fake guacamole and calling it the real thing.

So much of what gets passed off as love today is far less. And one of the most common counterfeits? *Tolerance.*

Tolerance says, "You do your thing, and I'll do mine."
Love says, "You matter enough for me to show up, speak truth, and stay."

Josh McDowell once put it like this:

> Tolerance says, "You must approve of what I do."
> Love says, "I must do something harder: I will love you, even when your behavior offends me."
> Tolerance says, "You must agree with me."
> Love says, "I will do something harder: I will tell you the truth, because I am convinced 'the truth sets us free.'"
> Tolerance seeks to be inoffensive.
> Love takes risk.
> Tolerance costs nothing.
> Love costs everything.

Tolerance may create space, but only love creates belonging.
Tolerance may let someone live, but only love helps someone live well.
Tolerance might leave you alone, but love will never leave you behind.

It's not that tolerance is bad, but it sure is an inadequate foundation for life.

The Scriptures never say:

> "*Tolerate* the Lord your God with all your heart, soul, and mind. And *tolerate* your neighbor as yourself."
>
> "For God so *tolerated* the world that he gave his only Son . . ."
>
> "If I speak in the tongues of mortals and of angels, but have not *tolerance*, I am a noisy gong or a clanging cymbal . . . *Tolerance* is patient, *tolerance* is kind . . ."
>
> "Friends, let us *tolerate* one another, for tolerance comes from God . . . for God is *tolerance*."

Why not?

Because God does not merely tolerate you. He doesn't glance in your direction with indifference or settle for keeping the peace. He looks at you—flawed, broken, beloved—and says, *Tolerance is not enough. I will move toward you. I will sacrifice for you. I will give my Son for you.*

As C. S. Lewis once said, "A world of nice people, content in their own niceness . . . would be just as desperately in need of salvation as a miserable world—and perhaps might be more difficult to save."

Niceness is not the same thing as the love of God.

Can you imagine a spouse telling another on their wedding day, "I promise to tolerate you"?

And just so we're clear, tolerance can be good. But it is a poor substitute for the kind of love that is genuine to the love of God: "Hate what is evil; hold fast to what is good; love one another with mutual affection; outdo one another in showing honor. . . . Rejoice in hope; be patient in affliction; persevere in prayer. . . . Bless those who persecute you. . . . Rejoice with those who rejoice; weep with those who weep. . . . do not be arrogant. . . . Live peaceably with all" (Romans 12:9–18 NRSVue).

This was the Scripture reading at my wedding. Not poetic verses or romantic aphorisms, but short directives about what genuine love looks like in motion. Because real love—the kind that endures and transforms and gives itself away—is not built on sentiment or clear boundaries. It's built on persistent sacrifice.

This is the kind of love I want to not only understand but become. This is the kind of love I still want to live.

Love That Brings You Back

Maybe that's why Romans 12 means so much to me.

Because for a long time, I didn't believe that kind of love was possible. After what happened in that Sunday school classroom in high school, I quietly walked away from church. No big announcement. I just slipped out the side door of faith, disillusioned and numb.

If *that* was love—if *that* was what Christians meant by it—I wanted no part of it.

What I didn't realize was that love doesn't give up so easily. Not God's love, anyway.

His love kept moving toward me, even when I wasn't moving toward him. Even in my skepticism, my distance, my confusion, God's love was still active. He was still pursuing.

And it came, not in dramatic moments or emotional breakthroughs, but through people.

Friends in college who didn't preach at me but walked with me.
A roommate who didn't judge.
An upperclassman who prayed with me and for me.
Mentors who made space for my questions without compromising the truth.

They didn't just *talk* about love—they *lived* it.

Their friendship had depth. Their welcome had no expiration date.

Through them, I encountered something I had almost given up on: genuine love. Not the flashy, worldly kind. Just a love that stayed and made room. Slowly, my heart began to soften.

Through them, I began to see Jesus again in the way they cared for and carried one another, not through a textbook or a theological argument.

That's what brought me back—God's love through them.

Love That Costs and Stays

So how do we move beyond counterfeit love and into something real?

How do we love in a way that draws near, that walks beside, that bears burdens and refuses to let go?

That's what happened when Lisa Fenn met Dartanyon and Leroy.

Lisa was an ESPN producer working on a human-interest story. Dartanyon and Leroy were two high school students—one legally blind, the other a double amputee—trying to survive in a struggling Cleveland school system.

What struck Lisa most was the way they moved. Dartanyon would carry Leroy on his back—up the stairs, into class, to the gym for wrestling practice, wherever they needed to go. One had eyes and the other had legs, and combined, they both had what they needed.

It wasn't just friendship. It was devotion.

Lisa planned to produce a brief segment about the two students and move on. But she couldn't forget them. The story aired, but her heart stayed behind in Cleveland.

She realized that *telling* a story about love wasn't the same as *entering into* one.

So, she moved into Dartanyon's and Leroy's lives. She helped them fight for scholarships and find housing. She stayed and walked with them through trauma, becoming like a second mother.

She gave them her presence, her persistence, her prayers.

Lisa didn't just write about love. She let love dwell in her. And through her, it changed the lives of two young men who'd had every reason to believe they were alone.

That's the kind of love God offers you. Not love from a distance. Not love in theory. Love that enters in.

John puts it like this: "This is how God showed his love among us: He sent his one and only Son. . . . This is love: not that we loved God, but that he loved us and sent his Son as an atoning sacrifice for our sins" (1 John 4:9–10).

God's love is not abstract. It's embodied. It has blood in its veins, scars on its hands, and a cross on its back. It's proved not by emotion but by offering. Not by affection alone but by atonement.

There's an old story from the Scottish Highlands about a shepherd who lost a ewe during lambing season. The lamb survived, but without its mother's scent, it was doomed. Other ewes refused to adopt it.

So, the shepherd took the fleece from the dead ewe and draped it over the orphaned lamb.

Now, when another mother sniffed the little one, she smelled her own. She let it come close. She accepted it fully.

Why? Because it was *covered*.

That's what John means when he says Jesus was sent "as an atoning sacrifice." Jesus didn't just have affectionate feelings toward us—he *covered* us. His death makes our welcome possible.

Jesus bore our sin, took our place, and made reconciliation possible. His life, death, and resurrection opened the way for us to be fully and freely welcomed by the Father.

The shepherd's orphaned lamb wasn't accepted because the ewe was fooled. She welcomed it because it bore the scent of a love that was already hers. In the same way, God doesn't pretend when he receives us. He isn't deceived. It's his own love—his own plan—that sent Jesus to bring us home.

And now, when the Father looks at us, he sees us wrapped in Christ, covered in grace, fully known and fully embraced.

As Paul says in Galatians 3, "For all of you who were baptized into Christ have clothed yourselves with Christ" (Galatians 3:27).

We are wrapped in his life. Covered by his love. Welcomed as his own.

Even in fiction, we glimpse this kind of love.

In the Harry Potter series, before Harry ever casts a spell or knows his own name, he is marked by his mother's love. Lily Potter stands between Harry and death, and her sacrifice becomes a shield. Her love doesn't just protect; it *lives* in her son. It gives him the strength to resist hatred and to lay down his own life for others.

That's the power of sacrificial love—to cover, to heal, to change.

And if that's what a fictional mother's love can do, how much more can the perfect love of God reshape our lives?

Love You Can Trust

Sometimes, after all the theology and all the stories, we're still left wondering.

Can I really trust this kind of love? Not just admire it. Not just define it. But lean the full weight of my life on it?

The theologian Karl Barth spent his lifetime exploring the depth and wonder of God's revelation. His *Church Dogmatics* stretched over six million words. His footnotes were longer than some books. His intellect shaped generations of scholars and preachers.

But near the end of his life, during a lecture tour in the United States, someone asked Barth if he could sum up all he had written—all the volumes, all the insight—in a single sentence.

Barth paused and then replied with a quiet smile: "Jesus loves me, this I know, for the Bible tells me so."

It wasn't a joke. It wasn't a deflection. It was the truest thing he knew.

After decades of study, after unpacking doctrines and wrestling with Scripture, he came back to what a child could sing: The love of Jesus is real. And it is for *you*.

A love that won't let you go. A love strong enough to save. A love deep enough to heal.

You don't have to fully understand it to receive it. You don't have to be worthy to be offered it. You don't have to clean yourself up first to have it.

You begin by receiving because this love is already reaching for you.

But the love of God doesn't just reassure—it reshapes. It invites us to live differently. Not to earn affection, but because we already have it. Not to impress God, but because his Spirit is already at work within us.

To trust his love is to participate in it.

It means letting your guard down and allowing grace to take root. It means moving toward people the way Jesus moved toward you—with patience, honesty, and sacrifice. It means showing up, staying when it's hard, and refusing to settle for sentiment when the world needs something stronger.

This is the journey we share.
Loved by God, we learn to love one another.
Together, we become people in whom love dwells and through whom love flows.

An Invitation for Reflection & Growth

KEY VERSE

Hatred stirs up conflict,
but love covers over all wrongs.
—Proverbs 10:12

BIG IDEA

Love is not merely a feeling—it's the first fruit of the Spirit and the foundation for all the others. It is expressed through obedience, loyalty, service, and endurance. Because God first loved us, we can love others in ways that are sacrificial, steadfast, and surprising.

READING & REFLECTION

Love That Obeys

Read Deuteronomy 6:4–9 and Proverbs 10:12

- Why is the greatest commandment to love God with all your heart, soul, and strength?
- How is love connected to obedience—not as duty, but as devotion?
- Where is God inviting you to love him by aligning your life with his heart?

Reflection & Practice

- Name one command of God you've been resisting. Choose to practice it today—not out of obligation, but as an offering of love.

Love That Remains

Read Ruth 1:6–18

- What is striking about Ruth's choice to stay with Naomi? Why is her loyalty so radical?
- How does covenant love differ from convenient love?
- Where might God be calling you to remain in love—even when it may be difficult?

Reflection & Practice

- Write the name of someone God is calling you to love with loyalty. Ask God for the strength to stay—and the grace to serve.

Love That Serves

Read John 13:1–17

- Why does Jesus wash his disciples' feet, and what does that teach us about love?
- What does it look like to serve someone in your own life and work? Consider both those whom you love and those you struggle to love.
- Where might pride, power, or position be keeping you from love?

Reflection & Practice

- Do one quiet act of service this week that no one except God sees. Let this secret become sacred ground.

Love That Never Ends

Read 1 Corinthians 13:1–13

- Why is love greater than gifts, faith, or knowledge?
- Which qualities of love (verses 4–7) are most challenging for you to live out?
- How does eternal love reshape your daily relationships?

Reflection & Practice

- Read 1 Corinthians 13 out loud each day this week. Ask God to grow lasting love in you, especially where it's most difficult.

CULTIVATION PRACTICE: TAKE UP THE TOWEL

In your journal or notebook, draw a simple towel. Nothing fancy, just a rectangle with four corners. This isn't about artistry; it's about intention. On each corner of the towel, write down:

- Someone who is easy to love
- Someone who is hard to love
- One way Jesus has loved you
- One way you can extend that love to someone else

Let this image become more than a sketch—let it be a visual prayer, a sacred reminder of the towel Jesus wrapped around his waist. The love that kneels. The love that washes. The love that serves even when it's not returned. May this towel remind you that love doesn't always look like grand gestures. Sometimes, it looks like small corners of faithfulness, held open in your hands.

A PRAYER TO CULTIVATE LOVE

Jesus,
Your love is not abstract or far away.
You moved toward me—before I ever moved toward you.
You saw me in my weakness, my failure, my fear—
And still, you stayed. Still, you gave. Still, you called me as your own.

I don't always trust love.
I've seen too many counterfeits.
I've hurt too many times.
But your love is different.
It covers. It heals. It holds.

So today, I say yes.

Yes to being covered in your grace.
Yes to being defined by your love.
Yes to sharing that love with others.

Jesus loves me, this I know.
That is where I begin and end.
And that is enough.

Amen.

CHAPTER 2

JOY

The One Who Gives You a Song

My wife and I once traveled to the Greek island of Santorini. Travel guide author Rick Steves says of its crescent-shaped coastline, "If you can't snap a postcard-quality photo here, it's time to retire your camera." Volcanic-forged black cliffs fall dramatically into sapphire-hued waves. Whitewashed homes and domed churches, stacked like an avalanche of sugar cubes, cling to the edge of the caldera, all pointing upward into the endless blue sky.

As we wandered the narrow streets, I started to notice something peculiar: Nearly every piece of property seemed to have a church. Not just in town squares or on main roads, but tucked beside homes, perched on terraces, hidden in gardens. And these weren't just big cathedrals—there were tiny chapels, large enough to hold only a few people. Some looked more like ornate closets than grand sanctuaries.

Curious, I asked a local cab driver what the story was.

“Every family builds a church on their land,” he explained with a wide smile and arms that gestured more than steered. “But not for weekly worship. These churches are storehouses—for celebration.”

He went on to explain that once a year, each family hosts a feast for the entire village. Their little chapel becomes the center of hospitality. Food is brought out. Wine is poured. Stories are told. And in a way that seems both sacred and utterly human, they turn the sanctuary inside out and throw a party.

“In my village,” he said proudly, “there are over twenty-two celebrations every year!”

Seeing my wonder, he leaned in and said, “Right now, our family church is storing more than one hundred bottles of my own wine—just waiting for the day of joy.” Then, lifting his hands high above the steering wheel, he shouted, “We open the doors of the church. We bring everything out. Everyone is invited. We celebrate!”

That’s a little different from the Christianity I grew up with.

We didn’t exactly throw parties in church. Lemon bars were about as much excitement as we allowed. Church was more somber than joyful—reverent, yes, but often heavy. I don’t remember hearing anyone say, “I can’t wait to open the doors and bring everything out.”

Somehow, in many corners of the modern church, joy has become optional. A footnote, even. A feeling reserved for Christmas morning or Easter brunch. In the meantime, we've lost something essential.

Joy is not a nice add-on benefit to faith. It is evidence of it.

Joy is not the result of easy circumstances. It is the fruit of a rooted life.

It's the second word on Paul's list, right after *love*. If love is genuine, how on earth does it not lead to joy? Joy is the thread that holds the Gospel of Luke together—from the silence of Zechariah to the joy of resurrection.

Maybe the best place to begin is not with an explanation of joy but with a story, a gospel story. Because the gospel is, quite literally, good news of great joy.

From Silence to Song

The Gospel of Luke begins in a strange silence.

A priest named Zechariah is chosen by lottery to enter the temple and offer incense. It's the high point of his long career—a once-in-a-lifetime opportunity. But instead of emerging with a triumphant word or a blessing for the people, Zechariah walks out mute. Silenced by unbelief. Overwhelmed by a promise he can't quite trust: that God is going to give him and his wife a son, even in their old age.

The people are left to wonder. Zechariah is left to wait.

His silence becomes symbolic of a nation waiting in the dark. Four hundred years without a prophet. Four centuries without a word from God. The temple still stands, but the joy is gone.

And then, everything changes.

The angel Gabriel visits a young girl named Mary. She's barely old enough to be married, certainly not expecting to have a child. And yet, when she hears the promise of God's coming Son, she doesn't respond with suspicion or silence. She bursts into song: "My soul glorifies the Lord and my spirit rejoices in God my Savior" (Luke 1:46–47).

It's the first clear sound of joy in this Gospel. Here's the voice of a young woman who believes that the promises of God are not only true—they're also good.

Joy is not the absence of trouble. Mary's life was about to get harder, not easier. She would carry a miracle and face trials. She would flee to Egypt, raise a misunderstood son, and one day watch him die.

But her song rings out anyway, because joy is not grounded in circumstance. It's grounded in something deeper.

Her song is joined by another, just a chapter later. The shepherds—minding their own business in the middle of the night—are interrupted by an angel with an announcement: "Do not be afraid. I bring you good news that will cause great joy for all the people" (Luke 2:10).

Good news of great joy. That's what God sends into the world.

Luke opens in silence, but it doesn't stay there. By the end of the Gospel, after the cross, after the resurrection, Luke tells us that the disciples returned to Jerusalem "with great joy" and were "continually at the temple, praising God" (Luke 24:52–53).

The story that began with a *speechless priest* ends with a *singing people.*

Because Jesus didn't come just to make you good. He came to make you glad.

He came to restore what sorrow had stolen.
To awaken what religion had muted.
To fill the storehouse of your soul with something worth bringing out.

Joy That Doesn't Expire

In our culture, joy is often confused with happiness. Money can buy happiness. It just doesn't last very long.

A tropical vacation, a great meal, a surprise upgrade to a better seat on a flight—these things can absolutely make us happy. And happiness isn't bad. God made us for delight. But happiness is fleeting; it runs out. It's shaped by our circumstances and how well things are going. It can evaporate with a single diagnosis, a pink slip, a critical comment, or a cracked phone screen.

That's why we need more than happiness. We need eternal and lasting joy.

The difference is simple: Happiness comes from what's around you. Joy comes from what's beyond you. Joy doesn't depend on the stock market or the weather or your kids' behavior in the back seat. Joy is rooted deeper. It's anchored in something the world can't touch.

People who experience joy are often, in fact, happier. But the reverse isn't always true. Chase happiness and you might miss both. Cultivate joy, and you may find happiness thrown in as a byproduct. Joy grounds you when circumstances shift. It outlasts mood swings and market crashes. It offers something happiness never can—resilience.

Intellectually, most of us get this. But when the wheels fall off—when the plans unravel or the prayers go unanswered—it's easy to forget. The things we once used as sources of strength start to feel like sand.

That's why Scripture keeps reminding us: "The joy of the LORD is your strength" (Nehemiah 8:10).

Not your wealth.
Not your security.
Not your adventure.
Not your perfect plan.

Real joy is not an accessory for the good times. It's an anchor for the hard ones. And that's exactly what we see in one of the most surprising moments in the book of Acts.

Does God really give us the ability to rejoice in all things? Is that even realistic?

In Acts 16, Paul and Silas were in the city of Philippi. They had cast out an evil spirit, healed a girl, disrupted a corrupt economy—and for that, they were beaten, arrested, and thrown into jail. The inner cell. Shackled and bloodied, isolated and in pain.

And what did they do?

They sang. "About midnight Paul and Silas were praying and singing hymns to God, and the other prisoners were listening to them" (Acts 16:25).

They didn't wait for the miracle to start rejoicing. They didn't praise God *because* they were delivered—they praised God *before* they were delivered.

They sang in the dark. They sang in the pain. They sang because joy doesn't depend on your surroundings—it depends on your Savior.

And then the miracle came.

The ground shook. The chains fell. The doors flew open. But the most powerful moment wasn't the earthquake. It was what came next. Because even though they were free to run, Paul and Silas stayed. And when the jailer saw that they hadn't escaped, he fell trembling at their feet and asked the question that only joy and freedom can provoke:

"What must I do to be saved?"

That night, the jailer and his whole household were baptized. The prison became a sanctuary. Suffering became salvation. And the joy of the Lord proved stronger than steel bars or locked doors.

Years later, Paul would write back to this same community—the Philippians—from another prison cell. Only this time, he wasn't the new convert. He was the one urging them to keep going. To keep trusting. To keep rejoicing.

"Rejoice in the Lord always. I will say it again: Rejoice! . . . The Lord is near" (Philippians 4:4–5).

Rejoicing is always possible. Not because it is easy, but because God is close.

Dallas Willard once offered me a simple but transformative exercise for cultivating joy. He challenged me to read one psalm of praise—just one—from Psalms 145 to 150, six days a week for several months. Then he said something I'll never forget:

"It's literally impossible to do that sincerely and not become a more joy-filled person. People train their muscles. Why do we think it's any different with joy?"

That moment lodged itself deep in my soul. It wasn't just advice; it was an invitation to practice joy as a discipline—something we train for, stretch toward, and grow into over time.

We don't drift into joy. Like any fruit of the Spirit, it takes practice, presence, and the persistent shaping of Christ. And I've found that as we give ourselves to that shaping, joy often surprises us—rooted deeper than circumstance, rising stronger than we expected.

My Grandfather's Joy

A few hours after my grandfather was buried, I quietly closed the door to his study. I wasn't looking to be alone so much as I was longing to feel close to him. The room still carried his scent—books and leather and something warm that I still can't quite name. I could almost see him there: Al Kannwischer, a thin man of medium frame, dark-rimmed glasses perched over kind eyes, a smile as warm as the sun, and snow-white hair that looked like it had been painted on with care.

I sat in his chair, the same chair where I used to climb into his lap as a boy, interrupting whatever serious thing he was working on. "You little imp," he'd tease me in his thick German accent. "I can zee da mischief in da corners of your eyes."

Everything in the study was just as he'd left it—the trinkets from his travels, the framed diplomas and awards, the rows of books he had actually read. My eyes eventually drifted toward the tall, metal file cabinets. For years I had wondered what was in them.

He had lived such an extraordinary life. Fled Germany as a young boy during the Great War. Survived a few harsh years in Russia during the Bolshevik Revolution. Immigrated to the United States at age fourteen. Taught himself English, excelled in school, and earned a PhD studying under theologians like Paul Tillich and even Dietrich Bonhoeffer. He had been one part pastor, one part professor, and one part prison chaplain.

I opened the first drawer and began flipping through a hodgepodge of manila folders. One in particular caught my eye. On the tab, written in my grandfather's careful hand, were the words "My Favorite Sermon." I opened the folder.

Inside was a treasure I knew I would cherish for the rest of my life: the manuscript of his favorite sermon, titled "Joy Above All Circumstance."

The message was built on Paul's letter to the Philippians. One passage was double-underlined: "I know what it is to be in need, and I know what it is to have plenty. I have learned the secret of being content in any and every situation, whether well fed or hungry, whether living in plenty or in want. I can do all this through him who gives me strength" (Philippians 4:12–13).

He had preached this sermon often. And he had lived it—through war and poverty, academic rigor and pastoral ministry, even when he was battling Parkinson's disease at the end of his life. As I held the faded pages, I realized something: I didn't yet know that secret. I had only recently returned to Jesus and to the church. I didn't know what it meant to rejoice in *all* things. But I wanted to. I wanted to live with the kind of joy my grandfather carried.

I wanted what he had—not his résumé, not his reputation, but his resilience. His deep, abiding joy.

He had lived through loss, disappointment, and displacement, yet somehow, joy never left him. It lived in him. And now, sitting in his study, I was learning what he had quietly passed on to me—not a formula, not a feeling, but a way of life.

When Paul writes of a "secret," it isn't something that's hidden from us—it's hidden *for* us, waiting to be discovered in the places we least expect it: prison cells and hospital rooms, unemployment lines and midnight cries. In the places where happiness withers, joy roots down deeper.

The secret to joy is not the perfect life. It's a person who gives you strength in every kind of life.

Because joy is not a reward for getting everything right. It's a fruit of the Spirit. It's what begins to grow when you stay rooted in the love of Jesus.

Joy That Shows Up Anyway

There's one more picture of joy I want to leave you with.

A friend of mine has a daughter who was preparing for her wedding. They were a well-known family, and the celebration was going to be held in a large church with hundreds of guests—the kind of wedding where every detail was carefully planned and every seat was filled with expectation.

The bride had been doing most of the preparation herself. Her fiancé, working out of state, kept calling with plausible excuses for why he couldn't get back to town early. And she slowly began to realize something was wrong.

Then, two days before the wedding, he told her, "I'm not coming." He wasn't going to marry her at all.

What do you do when your life turns from celebration to sorrow in an instant?

She cried, of course. Her family surrounded her with hugs, feeling her heartache. But then, through the grief, a strange conviction began to grow in her: *We're going to have the party anyway.*

Because for her, a wedding was more than a ceremony. It was meant to be a celebration of *God's* faithfulness, not just hers. Even if the groom failed to show, God had not. Even if the plan fell apart, love hadn't. The event wasn't just about what was happening *to* her—it was about what God was still doing *in* her.

So, they skipped the ceremony. But they went ahead with the reception.

Can you imagine that moment? Can you picture the courage it took to walk into a room full of people expecting a wedding and instead give them a witness?

The woman who was no longer a bride stood up, took the microphone, and thanked her guests for being there—not for the event they'd come to see, but for the joy they were now here to share. She honored her family. She pointed to God's presence. And then she said something that still echoes in my heart:

"It was all paid for anyway."

That is the source of our joy.

Not the kind that depends on how the story goes. But the kind that shows up anyway. The kind that blesses the table, even when the guest of honor never arrives. The kind that walks into the sorrow and still throws open the doors.

Do you see the overlap here between love and joy? Love means we are unconditionally accepted. Love means God does not let you go. *Joy is the grateful response to the love of God.*

It's the logical next step. Behind every glimmer of the love of God is a reminder of his delight in you.

The book of Hebrews tells us that "for the joy set before him [Jesus] endured the cross" (Hebrews 12:2). Think about that. The joy was not the cross itself—it was *you* on the other side of it. It was the heavenly family being gathered. It was the eternal party being prepared. And Jesus wants you to know, "It's all paid for anyway."

That same Spirit who grew joy in my grandfather—who filled Paul and Silas in prison, who filled Mary with song—is ready to grow joy in you.

Not an emotion you wait for, but a choice you walk in.
Not an accessory to your faith, but the evidence of it.

The first line of one of the old catechisms poses the ultimate question: *What is the chief end of man?* The response? *To glorify God and enjoy him forever.*

The "enjoy him" part always disarms me. Am I enjoying God? Not just his benefits, but enjoying God himself?

Let your soul become a storehouse. Let joy fill the empty places. Let silence become a song of praise. And when the world least expects it, open the doors wide. Bring everything out. Because joy—*real* joy—does not expire. It can't be stolen. It doesn't dry up with age.

It overflows—not because of what's happening around you, but because of who is within you.

You are his joy. He delights in you. He invites you to celebrate. Enjoy this life with him.

An Invitation for Reflection & Growth

KEY VERSE

A cheerful heart is good medicine,
but a crushed spirit dries up the bones.
—Proverbs 17:22

BIG IDEA

Joy is more than an emotional response—it's the resilient delight that comes from the presence and promises of God. It sings in sorrow, dances in celebration, and cries out when silenced. It strengthens us to persevere and surrounds us when we feel alone. True joy begins in God, and it never ends there.

READING & REFLECTION

Joy That Dances

Read 2 Samuel 6:12–23 and Proverbs 17:22

- Why does David dance before the Lord, and why does this bother others?

- How do you express joy in God? What holds you back from the freedom to experience joy in his presence?
- Where is God inviting you to rejoice with freedom?

Reflection & Practice

- Celebrate something God has done recently, even if it feels small. Let your joy be visible and use it as a testimony to his goodness.

Joy That Strengthens

Read Habakkuk 3:17–19

- What does Habakkuk rejoice in, even when everything seems lost?
- How is joy different from happiness?
- Why do you need to anchor your joy in who God is, not in what's happening?

Reflection & Practice

- Write a prayer of joy that celebrates what you know to be true about God, even amid the mystery of what remains unseen.

Joy That Finishes

Read John 16:16–24

- What kind of joy does Jesus promise in John 16, and how is it different from the world's joy?
- How does resurrection joy transform sorrow? How can it reframe your experience of loss?

Reflection & Practice

- Where is God birthing joy through something painful in your life?

- Take time to reflect on one sorrow or struggle that God has redeemed or is redeeming. Give thanks for it.

Joy That Surrounds

Read Hebrews 12:1–3

- Who is in your "cloud of witnesses"?
- How does remembering others give you strength?

Reflection & Practice

- Where do you need to practice perseverance, and how does joy lead the way?
- Name one person (living or passed) whose faith strengthens you. What about their life and faith journey do you hope people see reflected in you? What is one practice from their life you can incorporate into yours?

Joy That Cries Out

Read Luke 19:28–44

- Why does Jesus say the stones would cry out?
- What joy do you need to voice despite opposition or misunderstanding?

Reflection & Practice

- Where is God calling you to rejoice boldly?
- Praise God aloud today, even if it feels awkward. Don't let the rocks do your job.

CULTIVATION PRACTICE: SING ANYWAY

Joy isn't the absence of sorrow—it's the presence of God in the middle of it. Choose one worship song, hymn, or piece of music that lifts your eyes to God. Play it every day, especially when you don't feel like it. As you listen (or sing), reflect on these questions:

- What line stands out to you? Why?
- How is God inviting you to rejoice in him, not your circumstances?
- Where is joy beginning to take root? Is it a loud ensemble or a quiet whisper?

Let the song carry you. Let it remind you: Joy is deeper than the moment. And even if you're still waiting for your breakthrough, sing anyway.

A PRAYER TO CULTIVATE JOY

God, you are the source of all true joy.
You don't wait for everything to be perfect—
you show up right in the middle of our mess
with good news and great joy.

You rejoiced over your people then,
and you rejoice over me now.
Sometimes that's hard to believe,
especially when life feels heavy or silent or stuck.
But you haven't changed.
You're still the God who celebrates,
who surprises,
who saves.

So, help me pay attention.
Open my eyes to beauty I usually overlook.
Give me a heart that leans toward wonder.
Help me find reasons to laugh,
to be thankful,
to rejoice—even in the hard places.

When I'm tempted to settle for shallow happiness,
root me in something deeper.
Let joy take hold in me—
not because life is easy,
but because you are near.

Make me someone who carries joy
wherever I go.

May it be so!

Amen.

INTERLUDE

MEMORIZE THE LIST

Before we move any further, let's take a pause.

Go back to the beginning with me.

The fruit of the Spirit isn't something we manufacture. It's something God cultivates in us as we remain rooted in Christ. But like any good seed, it starts with something small—something planted, repeated, remembered.

So let me offer you the simplest possible first step:

Memorize the list.

That's it. Just begin by knowing the nine: "But the fruit of the Spirit is love, joy, peace, [patience], kindness, goodness, faithfulness, gentleness and self-control" (Galatians 5:22–23).

Write them down. Say them out loud. Repeat them when you wake up. Whisper them before a meeting. Pray them on your commute. Tape them to your mirror. Make them your phone's lock screen.

Make them a part of your language.

Why? Because words shape worlds. Naming the fruit each day is a way of tending the garden of your soul. It reminds you what matters. It plants truth where weeds of fear, hurry, and cynicism want to grow.

Even better, it prepares you for the moments you'll need them.

You'll be stuck in traffic and feel your anger rising. That's when the word *patience* comes back.
You'll scroll past yet another online argument. *Gentleness* will echo in your memory.
You'll face a difficult conversation and remember, *love first.*
You'll find joy hard to come by and pray: *Lord, bear your fruit in me.*

Some days you'll feel fruitful.
Other days you'll feel like a dried-up vine.
Say them anyway.

The repetition isn't magic. It doesn't earn you any brownie points. But it will help you keep the right things in mind.

That's why generations of believers have made a habit of keeping God's words *visibly* and *verbally* before them.

In the Old Testament, God gave this instruction through Moses: "These commandments that I give you today are to be on your hearts.

Impress them on your children. Talk about them when you sit at home and when you walk along the road . . . Tie them as symbols on your hands and bind them on your foreheads. Write them on the doorframes of your houses and on your gates" (Deuteronomy 6:6–9).

It's a vivid picture: Scripture not just studied by the people, but *surrounding* them—seen in doorways, felt on their hands, spoken in everyday moments.

The message is to keep what matters *in front of you*. Say it. See it. Share it. Repetition shapes remembrance—and remembrance shapes response.

In other words, make God's direction a part of your daily rhythm. Let it shape your rising and your resting, your coming and your going, your speaking and your silence. Let it dwell in you so deeply that it shapes your instincts.

Paul builds on this same truth in his letters. He tells the believers in Colossae, "Set your minds on things above, not on earthly things" (Colossians 3:2). To the Philippians, he writes, "Whatever is true, whatever is noble, whatever is right, whatever is pure, whatever is lovely, whatever is admirable—if anything is excellent or praiseworthy—think about such things" (Philippians 4:8).

You see the pattern. Fix your mind. Focus your attention. Fill your thoughts. And not just once, but over and over again.

Because what you memorize, you will meditate on.

And what you meditate on, you will begin to embody.

I learned this in a way I'll never forget during one of the first sermons I ever preached. I was still in graduate school—green and eager—and was invited to speak at a Sunday evening service in a long-term care facility for the elderly.

The small chapel was full. Most of the residents had been wheeled in from their rooms. Many were hunched over, some unresponsive, others clearly distracted. I stood up front and did my best, but I could feel it—I wasn't connecting. My illustrations fell flat. My voice didn't impact. And I could tell, with every passing minute, that I was losing the room.

I ended the sermon feeling deflated, embarrassed, and more than a little unsure of my calling.

But then something remarkable happened.

After the final "Amen," a nurse stepped to the front of the room and began to lead the residents in singing. Great hymns of the faith—"Amazing Grace," "It Is Well," "Blessed Assurance." One by one, voices that had been silent began to stir. Lips began to move. Eyes opened. And something changed in the room. They were alive again.

Then they began to say the Lord's Prayer, in full voice and unity. Then the Twenty-Third Psalm. Their minds knew what their bodies had forgotten.

It was a holy moment.

That evening, I learned something I've carried with me ever since:

What you memorize, you will remember.

What you remember, you will return to.
And what you return to, you will reflect.

If you're going to memorize something, make it matter. Make it eternal. Make it fruit that will last.

Start with the nine.

Love, joy, peace, patience, kindness, goodness, faithfulness, gentleness, and self-control.

Say them every morning. Let them echo in your mind throughout the day. Repeat them at night. And when the noise of life tries to drown out your identity, let this be the whisper you carry: *This is who I am becoming, by God's grace.*

CHAPTER 3

PEACE

The One Who Calms the Storm

Back in my previous church in California, we had just finished a long, prayerful visioning process. You know, one of those organizational exercises where you wrestle with big questions like "What are we really about?" and "What is important to us?" Eventually, we landed on some language we felt captured the heartbeat of our church. One of the phrases we came up with was: *Unfathomable Peace*. Big, bold words. Something only God could provide. We even printed this on banners, which we hung outside the building.

A few weeks later, totally out of the blue, our church office received a visitor.

Picture it with me: It's a normal weekday morning. The staff is answering emails, refilling coffee mugs, and pretending not to eat Sidecar donuts in front of each other. And in walks a middle-aged woman from the neighborhood. She isn't a church member, just someone who passes by our campus every day on her morning power walk. But this time, she turns off the sidewalk and comes straight through our doors as if she were on a shopping spree.

She walks up to the front desk, looks our receptionist square in the eye, and says, dead serious, "You all advertise peace. I don't have any. How can I get some?"

No small talk. No introduction. Just straight to the soul.

The receptionist blinks, calls someone from the leadership team, and says something like, "Uh . . . this one is for you."

So, we invite her in. And she sits down with one of my colleagues as she pours out her story—her stress, her restlessness, her ache for something solid and still inside of her. And that banner? That little phrase on the side of our building? It was like a homing beacon for her heart.

Maybe today you're a little like her. Perhaps not marching into a church office, but carrying the same question in your soul:

I don't have peace. How do I get some?

Sometimes, we think peace comes from calm seas and predictable days. We assume it means everything is finally under control. But the famous encounter of Jesus calming the storm says otherwise (see Mark chapter 4). It's one of the clearest pictures we have of peace—not as the absence of chaos, but as the presence of Christ.

That night on the Sea of Galilee, the disciples were in real danger. The storm was no metaphor. The waves were crashing, the boat was sinking, and they were convinced they wouldn't make it out alive.

And what was Jesus doing?

Sleeping.

Not because he didn't care, but because he wasn't afraid.

When they woke him in panic, he stood and said, "Peace. Be still." And creation obeyed.

But here's the part we often miss: The moment they became most afraid wasn't during the storm. It was after he calmed it: "They were terrified and asked each other, 'Who is this? Even the wind and the waves obey him!'" (Mark 4:41).

In that moment, they discovered that peace wasn't the result of calmer waters—it wasn't born from improved circumstances. Peace came from presence. Not just any presence, but the presence of the One who speaks, and the sea obeys. Jesus was there with them in the boat, just as he is with you now on your journey. The One who does not remove the storm, but instead enters into it, extending the invitation: "Peace, be still."

When Fear Prays

There's an old joke about a minister and a New York City cab driver who die on the same day and find themselves at the Pearly Gates.

Saint Peter greets the cabbie first. "Name?"

"I'm Nick," he says. "Taxi driver. Noo Yawk City."

Peter checks his list, smiles, hands him a silken robe and a golden staff, and ushers the cabbie into a palace for a home. "Welcome to the Kingdom of Heaven."

Then it's the pastor's turn. "I'm Randolph Jones. Minister of First Presbyterian for the past forty-three years."

Peter consults the list again. "Here's your cotton robe and wooden staff. You may enter." He's taken to a small apartment.

The pastor protests: "That man was a taxi driver! I am a pastor! How can this be?"

Peter shrugs. "Up here, we go by results. While you preached, people slept. While he drove, people prayed."

It's not a great joke. But it's funny enough because it's a little too true—not about results in heaven, but about fear.

Fear, it turns out, is one of the fastest routes to prayer.

There's a more serious moment I'll never forget—this one not in a pulpit or pew, but on a patch of dirt under the African sun.

I was leading a small group in Malawi, sitting on faded plastic chairs arranged in a loose circle. The group was made up of teenage girls who were smart, strong, and committed to their education because the alternative was being sold into marriage at the age of fourteen.

At one point, I asked them a simple question: "What scares you the most?"

Without hesitation, they said, "Lions."

Not metaphorical ones in fantasy literature.

Real lions.

Each of them walked miles every day on dusty roads and narrow trails to get to school. And every one of them knew someone personally who had been attacked by a lion. Some had lost friends. They were not scared of failing a test or missing a college deadline. They feared being eaten alive on their way to class.

And you know what?

They didn't need to be convinced to pray.

They were a prayerful bunch not because they were more religious than other people, but because they were more aware of their need.

That day in Malawi, I realized something: We live in a culture that prizes self-sufficiency. We surround ourselves with safety nets and insulate our lives with endless conveniences. And then we wonder why prayer feels optional. Why peace feels so rare. Why God feels so distant.

We've created an illusion of control—and when that illusion cracks, we don't know what to do.

But these teenage girls from Africa? They knew.

They lived with eyes open to danger and hearts open to God.

If you asked the disciples to recall their most terrifying moment following Jesus, I wouldn't be surprised if they said, "That night on the Sea of Galilee . . ."

When Jesus Terrifies You

Up until this moment in the Gospels, following Jesus had been relatively exciting. He healed a paralyzed man, cast out a few demons, and preached some provocative sermons. The crowds were growing, and the miracles were mounting. Nothing so far had made the disciples think that following Jesus might be dangerous—until the boat ride.

Now, remember, these weren't tourists. Some of the disciples were seasoned fishermen. They knew the Sea of Galilee. They had weathered storms on the water. But this one was different. Fiercer. Darker. Waves pouring over the sides of the boat. They couldn't bail fast enough. The vessel was sinking. They were afraid: "They were terrified and asked each other, 'Who is this? Even the wind and the waves obey him!'" (Mark 4:41).

The Greek phrase used here is *mega phobia*. They were not just scared—they were completely freaked out.

Because Jesus had stood up in the middle of the chaos and said, "Quiet. Be still."
And the wind obeyed.
The sea went flat.

Creation itself listened to him like a scolded child.

Who *is* this man?

The Fear That Brings Peace

In Scripture, the phrase "fear of the Lord" appears over 130 times. It doesn't describe panic, dread, or anxiety—but *awe*. A deep reverence that brings us to our knees in wonder, not worry.

The book of Proverbs tells us plainly: "The fear of the Lord is the beginning of wisdom" (Proverbs 9:10).

Note that wisdom begins but doesn't end here. However, it must be said that one of the surest signs that we haven't yet truly encountered the living God is that we live with *no fear of him*.
We've replaced reverence with casual spirituality. We've made God tame.

We want a god who's predictable.
But we have a God who's mysterious.
We want a god who fits into our life.
But we have a God who claims all of it.
We want a god who leaves us alone.
But we have a God who draws near and asks everything.

Author Mark Buchanan says it like this: "Our God is too safe. The safe god asks nothing of us, gives nothing to us . . . he never drives us to our knees in hungry, desperate praying and never sets us on our feet in fierce, fixed determination . . . A safe god inspires neither awe, nor worship, nor sacrifice."

And then comes the truth I never want to forget, from Oswald Chambers: "It is the most natural thing in the world to be scared, and the clearest evidence that God's grace is at work in your heart is that you do not panic. Yet the remarkable thing about fearing God is that *when you fear God you fear nothing else, whereas if you do not fear God you fear everything else.*"

There's a difference between neurotic fear and holy fear. Neurotic fear spins us into anxiety, fixating on what we can't control, magnifying threats, shrinking our world. It robs us of peace. But holy fear—the kind rooted in awe and reverence—does the opposite. It steadies us. It recenters us. When we fear God rightly, we stop fearing everything else. Healthy awe is not the enemy of peace; it's the beginning of it. Because lasting peace isn't found in safety or certainty; it's found in surrender to the One who holds all things.

Peace in the Pilot's Seat

It's easy to misread this scene: Jesus, asleep in the boat. The storm rages, the disciples panic, and Jesus is . . . napping?

But scholars note something fascinating: The place where Jesus was sleeping is called the pilot's seat, the seat of direction. While the disciples think Jesus is doing nothing, he's actually in the very spot of control.

So, they cry out, "Don't you care if we drown?"

That question still echoes today.

"Don't you care?" asks the exhausted mother of a special needs child.

"Don't you care?" asks the wife of an alcoholic who keeps relapsing. *"Don't you care?"* asks the overwhelmed student, the childless couple, the small business owner, the burned-out teacher.

Jesus doesn't answer with a lecture.
He doesn't give them a weather report.
He speaks.

"Peace. Be still."

And the storm obeys.

The Non-Anxious Presence

Here's what I missed for so long: Jesus doesn't just *teach* about peace—he *is* peace. He is the non-anxious presence of God in the middle of life's most terrifying storms. Wherever he is, peace is not just possible, peace is near. That means any version of peace apart from him is, at best, a temporary illusion. It may soothe for a moment, but it cannot last.

When Jesus stands up in the boat and speaks to the wind and the waves, he doesn't recite a prayer or invoke a higher authority. He talks to the storm the way a parent talks to disobedient child: calmly, firmly, and with unquestioned authority.

"Peace, be still." No pleading. No panic. Just power.

If we are ever to know true peace, it won't come through better planning or perfect conditions. It won't come through control. It will come through presence—*his* presence. The One who commands storms and stills the sea is the only One who can calm the chaos within us too.

Peace for the Upper Room

There's one more biblical scene we need to visit.

It's not on a boat, but in a locked room. Not during a storm, but after the crucifixion. These same disciples are hiding behind closed doors, gripped by fear, disillusionment, and the trauma of the cross.

And then, Jesus appears.

John tells us: "On the evening of that first day of the week, when the disciples were together, with the doors locked for fear of the Jewish leaders, Jesus came and stood among them and said, 'Peace be with you!' . . . And with that he breathed on them and said, 'Receive the Holy Spirit'" (John 20:19, 22).

He doesn't lecture. He doesn't scold. He breathes.

The One who calmed storms with a word now breathes peace into their anxious bodies. He fills the room with his presence—and their lungs with his Spirit. The same breath that brought life to Adam in Genesis is now offered again to frightened disciples who aren't sure how to go on.

The risen Christ gives them more than reassurance. He gives them *himself.* His breath. His Spirit. His life. His peace.

If peace feels elusive, like air you can't catch, remember this: It's not something you have to create. It's something you can receive. The One who breathes peace is still doing it today. Into fearful lungs and tight chests. Into panicked prayers and sleepless nights.

He breathes. And peace follows.

Peace can't be engineered.
Peace can't be purchased.
But it can fill you.

Peace doesn't stand alone. It grows in the soil of love and joy. Love is what anchors us, assuring us that we are seen, known, and held by God. Joy is what lifts us, reminding us that even in sorrow, there is something deeper and more durable at work. And peace? Peace is what settles us. It's the steadying presence that flows from knowing we are loved and rejoicing in that love. Without love, peace feels hollow. Without joy, peace feels temporary. But when love embraces us and joy wells up within us, peace becomes the natural fruit that follows.

That's why Paul doesn't list these fruits randomly. Love, joy, and peace are a kind of holy sequence. Love welcomes. Joy awakens. Peace remains. Together, they shape a life that is not only grounded but growing. A life that can breathe deeply, rest freely, and live fully even in the struggle.

My Own Storm

Several years ago, I went through the process of becoming the senior pastor of a different congregation. Let's just say, the process wasn't the smoothest. There were hurt feelings, disparaging emails, confused staff members, and at one point, I preached a sermon knowing some people were actively hoping I'd fail.

While the congregation cast their votes to decide if I would be their next pastor, I was sitting in the church basement with no cell service, no Wi-Fi, and no way of knowing what was happening on the floor above me. I spent three hours alone with God in what felt like my own little storm. I had risked my career, along with the opportunity to provide for my young family, by throwing myself into a tempest of a congregation in conflict. I later found out I'd walked into the sanctuary of this church with a 28 percent vote of no confidence before I'd even started the job. (For context, clergy friends tell me 10 percent is usually career-ending.)

And yet, strangely, I felt peace. Not because things were calm. But because I knew who was in the boat with me.

I tell you this not because I've mastered peace.
Far from it.
But because I've tasted it.

Jesus never promised smooth sailing. He promised something far more powerful—himself: "In this world you will have trouble. But take heart! I have overcome the world" (John 16:33).

He never guaranteed stormless seas. But he always promised a Savior.

If you find yourself crying out "Where is peace?" look again at the One who is in the boat with you.

He is not asleep because he is indifferent.

He is asleep because he is not afraid.

And if he is not afraid, then we don't have to be consumed by fear either.

Where's Your Gaze?

One time I was on a boat in the Mediterranean Sea, leading a tour that visited a variety of archaeological sites from the New Testament. I was with a group from our church, and we were transferring from a large cruise ship to a smaller tender boat to reach the shore. Even though the sky was clear and the sun was shining, the wind was strong that day—sharp, unexpected gusts that made the sea more unpredictable than you'd expect on such a beautiful afternoon.

The tender boat was basically a glorified lifeboat—small, enclosed, and sensitive to every wave that slapped against the hull. As we loaded in, we were packed shoulder to shoulder, wedged together in awkward rows that put us uncomfortably close to people we hadn't met before.

I found myself sitting directly across from a middle-aged woman from Ireland. She was angled slightly toward me, and I was facing her. It would've been a perfectly pleasant setup if we were sitting still. But with every lurch of the boat, I could see the color draining from her face. She was turning green, and I was sitting directly in her line of fire. I started praying—not for peace, but for personal safety and hygiene.

She was clearly not a seafaring woman. You could see it in her posture, hear it in her breathing. The anxiety was building. And then, with tears in her eyes, she asked me in her lovely Irish accent, "Why aren't you afraid?"

I think she expected me to say something about having grown up on the water or being used to boats, some line about coastal confidence. But that wasn't it.

The truth was, I was facing a different direction.

From her seat, all she could see were waves and wind. From mine, I could see the captain.

That was the only difference. I could see the person steering the boat. I could see his face. And he wasn't worried, not in the least.

He looked calm. In control. Peaceful.

And because *he* wasn't afraid, *I* wasn't afraid.

Later that day, I took a picture of the captain. I wanted to remember that moment—not just as a funny travel story, but as a spiritual reminder. Because that's what prayerfulness is at its core: It's about attention. It's about focus. It's about what (or whom) you're looking at.

You can stare at the waves. Or you can fix your gaze on the captain.

If you're experiencing worry and anxiety, that's okay. But the solution isn't to fixate more on your fear. The solution is to fix your eyes on the One who holds your life and your boat in his hands.

Keep your eyes on the captain. And let his peace come into you.

As Jesus said, "Peace I leave with you; my peace I give you. I do not give to you as the world gives. Do not let your hearts be troubled and do not be afraid" (John 14:27).

A Psalm for the Storm

Let me close with a psalm that gave me peace during my own pastoral transition. I prayed this a lot in that tech-starved basement—and in other moments of distress. I invite you to let this prayer into your anxious heart:

> Then they cried out to the Lord in their trouble,
> and he brought them out of their distress.
> He stilled the storm to a whisper;
> the waves of the sea were hushed.
> They were glad when it grew calm,
> and he guided them to their desired haven.
> Let them give thanks to the Lord for his unfailing love
> and his wonderful deeds for mankind.
> —Psalm 107:28–31

He is still the One who calms storms.
He is still the One who whispers peace.
He is still the One who guides us home.

Perhaps today you feel like that woman who walked into our California church office, having read the *Unfathomable Peace* banner and wondering how she could get some.

Maybe you're more like the disciples in the boat—caught off guard by a storm you didn't see coming, terrified by the wind and the waves, and even more unsettled by the power of the One who calmed them.

Or maybe you're like those girls in Malawi who walk each day through real danger and always begin with prayer—not because it's a spiritual exercise, but because it's survival.

Or maybe you're like that seasick woman in the Aegean, facing the waves, growing greener by the minute, asking the person across from her, "Why aren't you afraid?"

And perhaps the answer is the same for you as it was for me: It all depends on where you're looking.

The storm or the captain?

Peace doesn't always come from calm circumstances. It comes from knowing who is in control when the storm rages on.

You don't have to pretend the storm isn't real. You don't have to pretend you're not scared. But you do have to choose where to set your gaze.

You can worry, or you can pray.
You can fixate on the wind, or you can focus on the one who commands it.
You can spin inward with anxiety, or you can open your hands in trust.

You cannot do both at the same time.

So let this psalm become your prayer. Let it echo your cry in the boat.

Then they cried out to the Lord in their trouble—and he brought them out of their distress.

God calms storms to whispers.

He hushes waves.
He brings peace to anxious hearts and guides his people to safe harbors.

May you be glad when it grows quiet.
And may you discover—maybe even today—that his peace truly passes understanding.

And that the One who calms the storm still breathes his peace.

An Invitation for Reflection & Growth

KEY VERSE

Deceit is in the hearts of those who plot evil,
but those who promote peace have joy.
—Proverbs 12:20

BIG IDEA

Peace doesn't come from having fewer problems, but from knowing God is present in the midst of them. Peace isn't passivity; it's the courage to intervene, the power to calm storms, and the grace to live reconciled with others. True peace is cultivated by the One who still speaks to the winds and the waves—and to our anxious hearts.

READING & REFLECTION

Peace That Rises

Read John 20:19–23 and Proverbs 12:20

- What fears or locked doors does Jesus step through in this story?
- How does Jesus offer peace—not as an idea, but as a person?

Reflection & Practice

- Where is God breathing peace into you?
- Breathe deeply and slowly. Whisper, *"Peace be with me."* Let that be your prayer in every anxious moment. Consider doing this as a spiritual practice for a month.

Peace That Intervenes

Read 1 Samuel 25

- How does Abigail bring peace in the midst of rising tension? What can you learn from her example?
- What does it take to be a peacemaker, not just a peacekeeper?

Reflection & Practice

- Where is God calling you to speak with wisdom and act with courage?
- Name one situation of conflict or tension where you can offer grace. Ask God for boldness and humility, then have the courage to extend the grace you have been given.

Peace That Reigns

Read Colossians 3:12–17

- How does Paul describe the peace of Christ ruling in our hearts?
- What practices help peace govern your words, relationships, and rhythms?

Reflection & Practice

- Where do you need to let peace take the lead in your life? How can you bless others by leading with peace?
- Write one phrase or word from this passage that anchors you. Repeat it as a breath prayer this week.

Peace That Stills

Read Mark 4:35–41

- What storms are raging around or within you?
- How does Jesus respond to panic in the story?

Reflection & Practice

- Where do you need to hear, "Peace, be still"?
- Imagine Jesus asleep in your boat—calm, present, unshaken. Let that image carry you through your storms.

CULTIVATION PRACTICE: PLANT A SEED OF PEACE

Peace doesn't appear overnight—it's planted, watered, and tended. Take a moment of silence each day. Breathe deeply and reflect on a place of stress, conflict, or unrest in your life. Then grab a notebook or journal and . . .

- Write down one peacemaking action you can take this week.
- Write down one person who brings you peace.
- Write down one promise of God that steadies your heart.

Let these be seeds of peace. Trust the Spirit to bring the growth.

A PRAYER TO CULTIVATE PEACE

Jesus, you don't just offer peace—you *are* peace.
You step into storms and don't flinch.
You speak into chaos and things settle.
You meet anxious hearts with steady love.

Sometimes my mind runs faster than my faith.
I try to hold it all together,
to fix, manage, and plan my way to peace.
But it never lasts.
Not without you.

So I bring you the tension I've been carrying.
The thoughts I can't quiet.
The weight in my chest I keep trying to ignore.
Would you meet me here?

Help me take a deep breath and remember:
I'm not alone.
I don't have to control the waves.
I just need to stay close to you.

Slow me down when I want to rush ahead.
Hold me steady when I want to give up.

Let your peace settle deeper than my fears,
and shape the way I respond to the world around me.

Make me someone who doesn't just crave
the absence of conflict or a life of ease,
but who lives in you, walks with you.

You're here, and I trust you.

Amen.

CHAPTER 4

PATIENCE

The One Who Waits with You

When our children were four and five years old, our family moved to Southern California—just twenty minutes, without traffic, from "the happiest place on earth."

Walt Disney once said his vision for Disneyland was to create a playground where families could connect and be together. For us, it was exactly that. Disneyland became our playground. With annual passes, we could go almost any time. On a random Tuesday afternoon, I might pick up the girls from school and spend a couple of magical hours at the park, and then still get home in time for dinner.

It was prime magic season. Our daughters were at that perfect age when the characters still felt like real friends and Mickey ice cream bar calories could still be burned with fast metabolisms.

As we settled into our playground, we didn't just enjoy the magic—we mastered it. I'm a maximizer by personality. So, I turned Disneyland into a personal challenge. Back then, they used a paper FastPass system (now called Lightning Lane) so park visitors could strategically skip the long lines. You went to a kiosk, collected the little tickets that gave you specific return times, and then planned your day accordingly. It wasn't enough for me to have fun at Disneyland. I wanted to *win*.

And win we did. I figured out how to zig when others zagged. I knew which ride to start with, when to turn left instead of right, and how to map out our day like a general preparing for battle. I gamified the whole thing. We even had a mantra: *No more than fifteen minutes.* I'd shout, "How long do we wait?" and my girls would yell back, "No more than fifteen minutes!"

It was our creed. Our culture.

Until the day guests came to visit.

These out-of-town friends didn't want to conquer Disneyland. They wanted to savor it. And when they decided to wait in a two-hour line for a ride, I tried to be a gracious host. I stood in line. I smiled. But inside, I was dying. More than that, I was watching my children unravel—whining, complaining, asking why anyone would wait two hours for a ninety-second ride. They were behaving like, well . . . spoiled and entitled theme park insiders. And I turned to my wife, Kelly, and whispered, "Who raised these kids?"

She didn't say anything. Which, of course, said everything.

It wasn't Disney that had made them impatient. It was me.

I had trained them to expect a life of shortcuts. A life engineered to avoid waiting. But the real world doesn't run on FastPasses.

Not long after that, I came across something Lewis Smedes once said: "Waiting is our destiny. As creatures who cannot by themselves bring about what they hope for, we wait in the darkness for a flame we cannot light. We wait in fear for a happy ending we cannot write. We wait for a 'not yet' that feels like a 'not ever.'"

Smedes is right. Whether we're waiting in a line, waiting on healing, waiting for clarity, or waiting for God to act, life is full of "not yet" moments.

And maybe that's exactly why patience is a fruit of the Spirit—not just a nice personality trait, but a fundamental marker of spiritual maturity.

Because patience isn't just about handling delays. It's about how we relate to time, to control, and to God himself.

In a world addicted to immediacy, impatience often masquerades as progress. But hurry is often the enemy of love. Speed tramples what truly matters. The first casualty of a rushed life is usually compassion.

Patience, then, is not passive. It's a countercultural resistance to the tyranny of urgency. It's the Spirit's quiet revolution in us—training us to live at the pace of eternity rather than the pace of anxiety.

That's why it's core. That's why it's fruit.

Without even realizing it, we try to engineer around the unknown and the very practices training us for a life with God. We hustle. We gamify. We take pride in our ability to plan, produce, and press forward. But eventually, every one of us finds ourselves standing still in a space we can't control. A line we can't shorten. A longing we can't satisfy on our own.

It is pure fantasy to think life runs on fifteen-minute intervals. And the Spirit does not work like a FastPass.

Patience isn't just about enduring delays. It's about living in trust. Trusting that even in the waiting, God is present. Even in the silence, God is working. And even in the "not yet," the Spirit is cultivating something eternal in us.

Waiting Room

We all want to skip the line. We want to skip the seasons of uncertainty, bypass the pain, sprint ahead to the resolution.

James Gleick, in his book *Faster*, points out that in many modern elevators, the "door close" button doesn't actually do anything. It's a placebo—installed not to hasten the process, but to soothe our impatience. The doors are programmed to close automatically after a set time, regardless of how many times we jab that button. But we still press it. Repeatedly. Because waiting, even for a few extra seconds, feels intolerable.

We crave the illusion of control, even if it's a lie. And perhaps that's the deeper issue. Our resistance to patience isn't just about time;

it's about surrender. We struggle not because the wait is long, but because we're not in charge of how or when it ends.

But again and again in Scripture, we're invited not to shortcut the wait, but to embrace it. In fact, the command to *wait on the Lord* shows up forty-three different times in the Old Testament. That's not a subtle suggestion. It's a spiritual rhythm.

One of the most well-known of those forty-three times comes in Psalm 40: "I waited patiently for the LORD; he turned to me and heard my cry" (verse 1).

It sounds lovely in English, doesn't it? So composed. So calm. *I waited patiently for the Lord.* You almost picture someone sitting quietly in a rocking chair on the porch with a cup of coffee, whispering holy mantras.

But that's not what David wrote.

I don't often take issue with how our English Bibles translate the original Hebrew, but in this case, I think we lose something crucial in the smoothing out of the poetry. In Hebrew, the line is literally this: *"Waiting, I waited for the Lord."*

It's the same Hebrew word repeated twice in a row. This is a known literary technique, called apposition or repetition for emphasis. It doesn't just mean "I waited." It means *I waited and I waited and I waited.* I kept on waiting. I didn't stop waiting. I waited through silence. I waited through tears. I waited even when nothing seemed to be changing.

In other words, David isn't saying, "Look at me, God, I'm being so patient." He's crying out, "God, I've been waiting and waiting—what gives?"

This is a very different posture. It's not polished. It's persistent.

And that's what real patience looks like in Scripture. Not serenity, but *stick-with-it-ness*. Not spiritual perfection, but spiritual endurance. Patience is faith stretched across time. It's hope that refuses to die even when the silence stretches on.

Psalm 40 is a prayer about God meeting us while we're longing. It's a song sung by people who know what it feels like to wait and wait and wait—and still choose to believe that God will turn, that God will hear, and that God will come.

Maybe that's why we're told so often: *Wait on the Lord.*

Not because it's easy.
But because it's necessary.

The Pit

If you've ever seen the first season of *Parks and Recreation*, you might remember "the pit."

It's this giant, gaping hole in the middle of a neighborhood in Pawnee, Indiana, that was left behind after a condo project was abandoned. And it just sits there: ugly, overgrown, unsafe. People complain about it. Kids fall into it. It becomes a symbol of what's broken in the community. The entire premise of the first season is built around trying to do something about the pit.

It's a good metaphor for what waiting can feel like.

Sometimes in life, we find ourselves in a pit—stuck in a situation we can't fix, watching time go by, hoping someone will do something, *anything*, to move things forward.

And that's exactly the image David reaches for in Psalm 40: "He lifted me out of the slimy pit, out of the mud and mire; he set my feet on a rock and gave me a firm place to stand" (verse 2).

When David describes his season of waiting, he doesn't talk about being mildly inconvenienced or delayed. He describes being trapped . . . feet sinking, hands slipping, helpless and hopeless at the bottom of a muddy pit.

It's a famous image from Scripture and a deeply honest one. For David, waiting is desperate.

In the ancient world, cisterns and pits were used to trap animals—or people. Some of them still exist today. In fact, if you visit the region known as Dothan in the Holy Land, you can still see deep stone pits carved into the earth. One of those pits may very well have been the one used by Joseph's brothers that we read about in Genesis 37 when they threw him down and left him for dead.

Joseph, of course, was the beloved son of Jacob, the very man who had once wrestled with God through the long, dark night. Jacob knew something of struggle, of longing, of unanswered questions. And so did his sons. But their waiting would take a darker turn.

Jealousy, betrayal, and silence filled the space where love should have been. And into that silence, Joseph was cast, not only into a literal pit, but into a season of waiting that would stretch for years.

The pit for Joseph was literal and then symbolic.

Because from that moment on, Joseph's life became a long story of waiting.
Waiting in chains.
Waiting in prison.
Waiting to be remembered.
Waiting to be rescued.
Waiting to be reunited.
Waiting for the dream God gave him to come true.

And he's not alone. The Bible is full of both men and women who had to wait, and wait, and wait.

Consider Abraham. God promised him a son and then made him wait twenty-five years to meet Isaac.

Or Jacob, who waited seven years for the hand of Rachel, only to be deceived and wait seven more.

Or Moses, who went from the palace to the wilderness, waiting forty years in Midian as a shepherd before God called him back to Egypt.

Or Hannah, praying through her tears year after year before Samuel was born.

Or David himself, anointed as king when he was a teenager, only to spend years dodging spears and hiding in caves before ever sitting on a throne.

This is the pattern of God's people in our broken world:
A promise . . . and then a pause.
A vision . . . and then a valley.
A call . . . and then a long stretch of silence.

Even in the New Testament, the waiting continues.

There's the woman with the issue of blood—twelve years of doctors and disappointment before she finally encounters the healing touch of Jesus.

There's Simeon and Anna—elderly saints who spent decades in the temple, waiting for a glimpse of the Messiah.

There's the blind man who waited his whole life before Jesus touched him.

The paralytic at the Pool of Bethesda who waited year after year for healing.

Even those closest to Jesus had to wait—three long days of grief and confusion between Good Friday and Easter Sunday.

Waiting is not a detour in the life of faith. It *is* the life of faith.

If you find yourself in a season of waiting—waiting on a diagnosis, waiting for direction, waiting on a relationship to begin or to be restored—*God's timing may test your patience, but it will never stretch beyond his promise.*

You are not forgotten. You are not invisible. You are not alone, abandoned at the bottom of the pit.

Even if all you can see is a faint sliver of light above you, God sees you. Even if your prayers seem to echo back in silence, God hears you. Even if it feels like nothing is happening, God is still at work.

He may delay, but he never forgets.

What Happens During Waiting

First, we learn that God may delay, but he never forgets, and we train to remember God's holy promise of always remembering us. This practice is the holy act of holding covenant close, just as the people of God have always done—binding God's promises on their hands, inscribing them on their hearts. On our hands and our hearts.

But we also learn this: *The silence of heaven is not indifference. It is preparation.*

When we're stuck in a season of stillness—when the emails go unanswered, the doors stay closed, and the prayers seem to echo back empty—it's easy to assume that God is distant. That he doesn't care. That he isn't listening.

But waiting is never wasted in the hands of God.

Psalm 40 takes a surprising turn after David's rescue. You might expect him to erupt in immediate gratitude for his changed circumstances. But instead, what emerges is something deeper. Something internal. Something that couldn't have been formed anywhere else but the pit:

> Sacrifice and offering you did not desire—
> but my ears you have opened—
> burnt offerings and sin offerings you did not require.
> Then I said, "Here I am, I have come—
> it is written about me in the scroll.
> I desire to do your will, my God;
> your law is within my heart." (verses 6–8)

David had grown up in the sacrificial system of his faith: day after day, burnt offerings and sin offerings stacked one upon another. All the rituals meant to bridge the gap between heaven and earth.

But in the silence and waiting, David realizes something profound: *That's not what God was really after.*

What God wants is not more sacrifices. He wants *us*.

He wants a heart formed by his Word, not just a life decorated with religious activity. And sometimes, it takes the stillness of waiting—the helplessness of being unable to produce, perform, or perfect anything—to finally hear that.

That's what happened to David. That's what happens to us.

We like to think we're more sophisticated than Old Testament Israel, but we have our own system of sacrifices, don't we?

We perform. We hustle. We optimize. We offer sacrifice after sacrifice in the hopes that our productivity will earn security, recognition, or control.

But what happens when we can't play the game anymore?

What happens when the metrics no longer matter, when we can't produce or perform or be "useful"?

That's when grace meets us. That's when the silence is no longer a void, but a voice. That's when we realize that waiting isn't punishment. It's preparation.

I am not minimizing the pain or dismissing the hurt of what appears to be unanswered prayers.
But remember, God cares more about what's happening *in* us than what's happening *to* us. Who we are becoming is more important than the present situation. Qualities like love and joy, peace and patience, cannot grow through immediate gratification.

God's work is often slow—deliberately so.

Not because he's absent or indifferent, but because real transformation takes time. He moves at the pace of formation, not fabrication. He is cultivating something that can't be microwaved.

That's why patience is essential. Because if we don't trust the slow work of God, we'll rush to force fruit that isn't ready—or we'll walk away before the harvest comes.

Pierre Teilhard de Chardin once wrote, "Above all, trust in the slow work of God."

The Spirit grows us slowly, like seeds in the soil. And while we may crave the fast and the flashy, what God desires in us is rooted, resilient character.

If you're willing to wait—if you're willing to let the silence do its work—what you'll discover is not just deliverance.

Because in the hands of God, *deliverance always turns into doxology.*

A New Song

First, we learn that God may delay, but he does not forget.
Then we learn that the silence of heaven is not indifference—it is preparation.

And finally, Scripture reveals this: *God's deliverance gives birth to praise.*

Psalm 40 says it this way: "He put a new song in my mouth, a hymn of praise to our God. Many will see and fear the Lord and put their trust in him" (verse 3).

Waiting gives way to worship.
Desperation gives way to declaration.
The pit gives way to praise.

I will never forget the day I walked into the common area of a hidden dormitory in India. Our church partners with an anti–human trafficking organization that shelters and rehabilitates girls—some as young as eight—who have been rescued from horrific abuse. As a father of two daughters, I could barely hold the reality of it. The pain. The injustice. The loss of childhood.

They didn't speak English. I didn't speak their language. But then I heard them singing the melody.

"What a friend we have in Jesus . . ."

Their voices floated through the room, fragile and strong all at once. These girls, who had every reason to despair, were praising from the pit. They were holding on to Jesus, not with sanitized sentiment, but with raw, defiant hope.

> Are we weak and heavy-laden,
> Cumbered with a load of care?
> Precious Savior, still our refuge—
> Take it to the Lord in prayer;
> Do thy friends despise, forsake thee?
> Take it to the Lord in prayer;
> In His arms He'll take and shield thee,
> Thou wilt find a solace there.

Tears filled my eyes.

They were still waiting. Still trusting. Still singing. In their voices, I was given a picture of faith-filled patience that echoes in my soul.

Because that's what God does. He doesn't just lift you out of the pit, he gives you a song to sing to take you to the other side.

Do you see how love and joy and patience are not separate categories, but deeply connected?

Again, it's not the fruits of the Spirit—plural. It's the fruit of the Spirit—singular. All of this grows together.

Patience is shaped by love: Without love, our waiting turns into resentment.
Patience is steadied by joy: Without joy, our waiting feels hollow.
Patience makes room for peace: It slows us down enough to notice that Christ is present in the storm.

In that way, patience helps link what we believe to how we live. It holds space for everything else to grow.

And yes, it's a gift—but it's also a muscle.

Like every fruit of the Spirit, patience grows through practice. When you slow down and open yourself to God's presence—when you practice listening, waiting, or Sabbath-keeping—you are joining the Spirit in cultivating this fruit.

So don't just ask for patience.
Make room for it.

The Pit Is Not Your Permanent Address

But let me clarify something important with a different kind of song.

When I say, "The pit is not your permanent address," I don't mean that waiting is always passive. I don't mean that we should sit quietly in the corner until life improves or God shows up. Waiting on the Lord is not spiritual laziness. It's not fatalism. And it's definitely not denial.

I learned this lesson early in life, though I didn't love how it was delivered.

When I was growing up, my mom used to sing this little tune from a cheesy children's musical we performed at church:

> Have patience, have patience, don't be in such a hurry.
> When you get impatient, you only start to worry.
> Remember, remember that God is patient too.
> And think of all the times when others had to wait on you.

She sang it with conviction. I *heard* it with irritation.

I hated it—especially when she'd sing it just as I was being demanding or entitled. And sure, I knew there were moments when I needed that reminder. Moments when I needed to trust more, push less, let go of control.

But even then, I also sensed: There are *other* times.

Times when patience can turn into passivity. When waiting needs to be active, intentional, even persistent.

Max Lucado puts it this way: "We are to wait—not so vigilant that we lose our patience, and not so patient that we lose our vigilance."

That's why I want to remind you: *Yes, wait on the Lord—but don't fall asleep in your waiting.*

In Luke 18, Jesus tells the story of a persistent widow who comes again and again to the unjust judge until he finally relents. It's a story not just about justice, but about a kind of holy defiance—about faith that refuses to give up.

It's also why Simeon's story in Luke 2 is so compelling.

Simeon is an old man, faithfully waiting for the coming of the Messiah. He's not checking out. He's not scrolling endlessly. He's not giving up hope. He is, as the text says, "righteous and devout . . . waiting for the consolation of Israel" (verse 25).

The Greek word for "waiting" there is *prosdechomai*. It combines *dechomai* ("to wait") with *pros* ("forward"). Literally: He was "waiting forwardly." The grammar may be clunky, but the image is perfect.

He was not just sitting around. He was leaning in. He was *looking forward* to what God would bring.

And here's what I want to say gently but directly: Some of you are in danger of losing your vigilance. You've been waiting so long, the edges of hope have started to fray. You're tempted to give up on the dream, to walk away from the relationship, to stop praying the same old prayer.

If that's you, hear the whisper of the Spirit: *Don't give up just yet. Don't walk away. Don't stop.*

Others of you are in danger of losing your patience. You're trying to force things that aren't ready. You're striving, grasping, engineering the outcome. And maybe the word you need is: *Relax. Trust. I haven't forgotten about you.*

Waiting well requires both vigilance and patience. A forward-leaning trust and a calm surrender.

Take a Walk with a Turtle

That brings me to one last story.

Bruce Feiler is a best-selling author and the father of twin daughters. Years ago, he was diagnosed with bone cancer in his leg. His daughters were just three years old. The man who wrote *Walking the Bible* suddenly couldn't walk at all. Surgery and treatment took away his ability to stand, let alone travel, run, or live a life he had once known.

Eventually, he was able to get around on crutches. And in that season, he wrote an article called "A Father's Prayer for His Children." In it, he reflected on what he was learning from the slower pace of life. It's worth quoting the whole thing: "The simplest consequence of walking on crutches is that you walk slower. Every step must be a necessary one. When you hurry, you get where you're going, but you get there alone. When you go slow, you get where you're going, but you get there with a community you've built along the way.
At the risk of admission: I was never nicer than when I was on crutches."
Feiler was forced to slow down and in doing so found the unexpected: A community.

In the 1840s, as walking shifted from a necessity to a leisurely pursuit across European cities, a new figure emerged on the streets of Paris: the *flâneur.* This urban wanderer was not in a hurry. He strolled the arcades and boulevards with no fixed destination, observing the rhythms of life with unhurried curiosity. One whimsical emblem of this slow-paced lifestyle was the peculiar fashion among some *flâneurs* to walk turtles on leashes, allowing the animal's deliberate, measured pace to determine their own. It was idleness as protest, slowness as art.

There's something about that image that has always stayed with me. As a quiet ode to moving slowly, it has become more than a historical footnote—it's grown into a personal hope for not only myself but my loved ones. In a world that worships speed and efficiency, I find myself longing for my daughters to become a little like the *flâneur.* Not aimless, but attentive. Willing to let wonder set the pace. Willing, even, to walk with the turtles.

Take a walk with a turtle. And behold the world in pause.

That's patience.

Not just waiting—but *beholding.*
Not just enduring—but *noticing.*

I love the image—take a walk with a turtle. Picture it on a leash at Disneyland.

And remember—
The One who calls you to wait is also the One who walks with you.
Even in the silence.
Even in the shadows.
Even in the pit.

His promises are still true.
His deliverance is still on the way.
Even now, even in the waiting, even when nothing seems to be happening.

You can't gamify your way out of the waiting.
You can't engineer a shortcut to blessing.
But you can learn to pray like David in Psalm 40.

You can sing from a hidden dorm that became a sanctuary.

He will meet you in the darkness.
And he will not delay forever.

An Invitation for Reflection & Growth

KEY VERSE

Whoever is patient has great understanding,
but one who is quick-tempered displays folly.
—Proverbs 14:29

BIG IDEA

Patience isn't passive—it's hopeful endurance. It waits with trust, not resentment. It doesn't demand control but leans on the strength of God in seasons of delay, longing, or silence. True patience grows best in relationship—with the One who waits with us and for us.

READING & REFLECTION

Patience That Longs

Read John 5:1–9 and Proverbs 14:29

- What do you notice about the man's long wait for healing? How do you relate to his struggle?
- Where in your life are you still waiting for movement or healing?

Reflection & Practice

- Why is patience so difficult in today's environment?
- Name one place where longing has worn you down. Invite Jesus to meet you in the wait—not just at the finish line.

Patience That Laughs

Read Genesis 18:1–15; 21:1–7

- Why does Sarah laugh? What does her laughter reveal?
- What happens when God finally fulfills what he promised?

Reflection & Practice

- Have you ever found yourself in a situation where you were tempted to give up waiting on the Lord? What spurred you on? Where did you find hope?
- Remember one time when God came through—after you thought it was too late. Give thanks and cherish that memory.

Patience That Perseveres

Read James 5:7–11

- What images does James use to describe patient faith?
- Where do you need strength to endure—not just today, but for the long haul?

Reflection & Practice

- Where in your life is patience most difficult to practice right now?
- In what area might God be gently forming you through delay, waiting, or frustration? Choose to stand in the longest line at the store. Take the slower lane on your drive. Let these ordinary moments become sacred spaces—opportunities to rest in God's

patient love for you and to practice extending that same grace to yourself and others.

Patience That Renews

Read Isaiah 40:27–31

- What promises does Isaiah give to the weary? What do these promises mean to you?
- What does it mean to "wait on the Lord" in Isaiah? What does it mean in your life?

Reflection & Practice

- Where are you exhausted? What would it look like to receive strength instead of striving?
- Write the word *renew* somewhere where it's visible this week. Let that word shape your posture, your pace, and your prayers.

Patience That Waits Together

Read Acts 2:1–13

- What were the disciples doing while they waited for the Spirit?
- How is waiting different when we do it in community?

Reflection & Practice

- Where might God be preparing something powerful in your shared prayers?
- Reach out to someone and say, "Let's wait on God together." Pray with them or for them this week.

CULTIVATION PRACTICE: SLOW YOUR STEP

This week, choose *one ordinary activity* to do more slowly—on purpose. Not to be productive. Not to finish it better. But simply to practice presence. Here are a few ideas to consider:

- Take a walk without headphones or your phone—just your breath and the sound of the world, moving at turtle speed.
- Enjoy a meal without screens, scrolling, or multitasking. Let it nourish more than just your body.
- Engage in conversation without rushing to respond. Listen as if love depends on it.

As you move through this slowed-down space, reflect on these questions:

- Where in my life am I trying to force growth?
- Where might God be inviting me to wait—and trust instead?

Patience doesn't just grow in stillness. It grows in *surrender*—when we release our grip on the outcome and choose instead to walk at God's pace. Let this practice be a quiet protest against hurry, and a way of saying with your body: *I trust the One who's not in a rush. I trust the journey.*

A PRAYER TO CULTIVATE PATIENCE

God, I don't like waiting.
I like fast answers, clear plans, quick results.
But you don't seem to be in a hurry.

You move at the pace of love,
and love is patient.

Teach me to slow down.
Not just in my schedule,
but in my spirit.
When things take longer than I want—
when people don't change fast enough,
or prayers feel unanswered—
help me not to give up or lash out.

You are patient with me.
Every day.
You don't rush my growth.
You don't scold when I stumble.
You walk with me, gently and faithfully.

So help me show that same grace to others—
and to myself.

Grow something deeper in me
than acceptance or endurance.
Grow trust.
Grow steadiness.
Grow the kind of patience that stays rooted
even when I want shortcuts.

Remind me that waiting isn't wasting—
not when I'm waiting with you.

Amen.

INTERLUDE

THE BROKEN BIKE

Before we go on, I want you to imagine a warm Saturday morning in late spring. You're out for a walk, coffee in hand, no real agenda. Just enjoying the beauty of the day. You're only a few houses down the street when you see it.

A kid sits at the edge of a driveway. His bike is tipped over beside him, one wheel still spinning like it hasn't realized the ride is over. You didn't see the fall, but his face is flushed—not from the sun, but from frustration. Maybe even shame. A scraped elbow, a drooping helmet strap, and a silent stare at a busted chain.

You pause.

"You okay?" you ask.

No response. Just a sniff and a stare.

You kneel down. The chain's slipped, the back wheel is a little bent. Nothing you can't help with. You walk back to your garage, grab a few tools, and return. You may not know the kid's name, but you know what love would do.

That's *kindness.*

Kindness doesn't wait for a connection or a thank-you. It sees a need and moves toward it. It's love in work boots—helping, fixing, noticing. It bends low and gives what it can.

While you're working, something else catches your eye. At the end of the street, a small group of older kids is watching—and laughing. Too loud. A little too mean. One of them shouts something that makes it clear: They're the reason that bike's broken in the first place.

Now there's a different stirring in your chest.

You stand up. Walk over. Not to shame or escalate, but to speak. Calm and clear. You call out the cruelty, saying what needs to be said. There's a wrong that needs to be addressed. You draw a line where none had been drawn.

That's *goodness.*

Goodness doesn't just offer help—it offers justice. It defends. It risks discomfort. It tells the truth, even when it would be easier to stay quiet. Goodness is love with a backbone.

When you return, the boy is still there. The bike is fixed and the trouble has passed. But he's still on the curb, quiet and unsure.

You don't rush him. Instead, you simply sit down beside him.

You ask him his name and what his favorite cartoon is. You listen more than you speak. And you wait—not just until he gets back on the bike, but until his shoulders relax and his eyes look up again.

That's *gentleness.*

Gentleness doesn't rush in with answers. It doesn't force healing or hurry people forward. It's quiet strength, held back in love. It makes room for someone else to breathe.

Sometimes the fruit of the Spirit looks like kneeling beside a broken bike.
Sometimes it looks like standing up.
Sometimes it looks like sitting down.

Kindness helps. Goodness intervenes. Gentleness listens.

All three come from the same Spirit.
All three are expressions of God in you, just a different facet of the beauty of his character.

As we've walked through the early fruit of the Spirit—*love, joy, peace, patience*—we've seen how each is distinct but deeply related. These are qualities we intuitively recognize and rarely confuse with one another. Love is the wellspring. Joy sings. Peace settles. Patience waits. They flow naturally one into the next, each with its own unmistakable shape.

But now we enter a stretch of the list that's easier to tangle.

Kindness. Goodness. Gentleness.
They sound similar. They often show up in the same moments. They all whisper instead of shout.

Yet in the New Testament Greek, they are clearly distinguished. And in the life of Jesus, we see each one exercised in a way that teaches us how to cultivate them—not just as vague virtues, but as embodied practices.

Before we explore each of them in depth, we must take a moment to pause.

Don't rush past them.
Don't blend them together.
Don't assume they're all just a form of "being nice."

Because they're not.

They are the Spirit's way of helping us *navigate how to love well in real life*—when someone is hurt, when someone is wronged, and when someone needs more than a quick fix.

Kindness shows up with help.
Goodness shows up with courage.
Gentleness shows up with presence.

Together, they are the soul's tool kit for showing love in everyday moments.

Broken Lives

If you want to see all three in motion at once, look no further than the story in John 8. A woman is dragged into the temple courts—caught in the act of adultery, thrown at the feet of Jesus, surrounded by religious leaders eager to make her shame a spectacle.

They demand judgment. They quote the law. They try to trap Jesus with their cruelty cloaked in righteousness.

And how does he respond?

First, he bends down and begins to write in the dirt. We don't know what he wrote, but we do know that in doing so, he drew attention away from their hate and back toward the ground, back toward humility. It was an unspoken act of *kindness*—de-escalating the moment, shielding her from their eyes, shifting the spotlight off her shame.

Then, Jesus stands and speaks: *"Let any one of you who is without sin be the first to throw a stone at her."*

He doesn't ignore the wrong. He doesn't sidestep justice. He names their hypocrisy. He confronts the system that punishes the vulnerable and excuses the powerful. That's *goodness*—love with a spine, truth with courage.

And finally, when they all walk away—stone by stone, footstep by footstep—he turns to the woman and says, *"Neither do I condemn you. Go now and leave your life of sin."*

That's *gentleness*. No lecture. No shame. Just mercy and truth woven together. He restores her with dignity and sends her forward in grace.

This is the Jesus we follow.
This is the Spirit who lives in us.
And this is the kind of love the world is starving for.

God is not only the one who completely helps and heals what is broken in the world. He is also the One who invites us to do the same, in his Spirit and in his way.

And with that, let's begin with the first of the three: *kindness.*

CHAPTER 5

KINDNESS

The One Who Pours Out

Pastor Louis Zbinden was leaving the First Presbyterian Church of San Antonio late one night. He had just finished an evening Bible study at the downtown church. As was often the case, he was one of the last to leave. On his way out, he encountered a man on the church steps—disheveled, possibly drunk, asking for a handout. Louis, tired and wary, brushed him off with a wave and a few dismissive words: "Go away. Buzz off."

A Blue Norther swept into South Texas later that night, one of those sudden cold fronts that blows in with biting wind and temperatures that drop faster than expected.

The next morning, Louis was the first one back for an early meeting. The cold had not relented. And there, on the front steps of the church, lay the same man—lifeless. He had died during the night, exposed and alone. And Louis was the one who found him.

He would speak of it often in later years, not to excuse it, but to confess it. To remember. And to bear fruit that would last.

Through his grief and repentance, a new resolve emerged. Louis and the church immediately mobilized. What began as a temporary warming shelter soon became something more permanent—a ministry of kindness that would go on to become SAMM (San Antonio Metropolitan Ministry), one of the leading homeless shelters in the region. Thousands have found food, safety, housing, and hope because of what God did in the wake of that tragedy.

An act of unkindness was transformed into an extraordinary and enduring act of kindness.

Because that's what the Spirit does. He turns things around. He convicts, restores, and cultivates something deeper. What we tried to brush off, he plants. What we once ignored, he waters. And over time, what seemed like a moment of shame becomes soil for a different future.

The Kindness That Changes Us

There's a verse tucked into Paul's letter to the Romans that rarely gets top billing, but it holds the weight of heaven behind it: "Do you not realize that God's kindness is meant to lead you to repentance?" (Romans 2:4 NRSVue).

Not shame. Not judgment. *Kindness.*

We often assume that what changes people is pressure or punishment. We tighten the rules, raise the stakes, clarify the incentives, make the consequences clear. But God tells a different story. His kindness—not his condemnation—is what softens the human heart. Kindness is what opens the door to repentance. Not false repentance that's driven by guilt or fear of getting caught, but the real kind where your heart turns, your eyes lift, and your soul begins to walk in a new direction.

That's what happened to Louis. One night, his unkindness brushed a man aside. The next morning, kindness began to rise from the wreckage. Not as a cheap cover for what had gone wrong, but as fruit born from sorrow. And it didn't just change Louis; it changed a city. That's how the Spirit works. When the seed of repentance is buried in the soil of grace, kindness grows.

Kindness, real kindness, is one of the most compelling and inarguable and disarming forces in the world.

We don't forget it when we see it. We stop in our tracks when we experience it. Sometimes we crumble under the weight of it because it shows us who we really are and who we might become.

Think of the last time someone was unexpectedly kind to you. Maybe you were rude or distracted, and they responded with grace. Maybe you were broken, and they didn't turn away. Maybe you were in the wrong, and instead of punishment, they offered presence. That type of kindness doesn't let you go. It haunts you in the best way. It makes you want to change.

Because kindness doesn't come from us. It comes through us. It is the fruit of the Spirit—not the product of a particular character type.

The Kindness You Can't Earn

John Ortberg tells the story of a boy named John Gilbert. John had a rare form of muscular dystrophy (Duchenne's disease), and with that disease you lose different abilities over time. First, he lost the ability to run. Then, he could no longer walk. Eventually, he could no longer feed himself. His body slowly became a prison.

John was invited to a fundraising gala one evening, a charity auction. At one point in the evening, a basketball came up for bid, signed by his favorite NBA team. As soon as it was announced, John noticed Gilbert's body jolted with excitement. His hands flailed uncontrollably in his wheelchair until his mother, with gentle but swift restraint, pulled his arms down. She couldn't let him bid. She couldn't afford it. Not even close.

The bidding took off quickly. Then a man in another part of the room placed a bid so high it silenced the crowd. The auctioneer counted down. The gavel slammed. *Sold.*

But the man didn't return to his seat. He walked straight across the room, picked up the ball, and gently placed it into Gilbert's hands—hands that would never dribble, never shoot, never play a game. But hands that could hold a treasure. And cherish it.

Ortberg reflects: "It took me a moment to realize what the man had done. I remembered hearing gasps all around the room, then thunderous applause and weeping eyes. To this day, I'm amazed. Have you ever been given a gift that you could never have gotten for yourself? Has anyone ever sacrificed a huge amount for you without getting anything in return?"

This is the kindness of God.

It is not a transaction. It is not a reward. It is an unexpected grace. One we could never earn. One we can only receive.

"*But when the kindness and love of God our Savior appeared*, he saved us, not because of righteous things we had done, but because of his mercy. He saved us through the washing of rebirth and renewal by the Holy Spirit, whom he poured out on us generously through Jesus Christ our Savior, so that, having been justified by his grace, we might become heirs having the hope of eternal life" (Titus 3:4–7, emphasis mine).

God's kindness appeared. He moved across the room of our helplessness. He placed in our hands a treasure we could never afford. And when the Spirit cultivates kindness in us, we're not simply being empathetic. We're extending to others the same astonishing grace we have received.

What Kindness Isn't

We often get kindness confused with politeness. We tend to think of it as a form of good manners. Yet kindness is not about being nice or having some artificially positive veneer we paste on to make people feel comfortable or to avoid conflict.

True kindness is not weak. It may be warm, but it is not shallow. It is fierce in its willingness to show up for others, to bear burdens, to pursue the good of someone else even when it costs you something.

And despite what coffee mugs and bumper stickers may suggest, kindness is not random.

We live in a world starving for real goodness. We long for mercy, truth, and healing . . . for a world made right. But in that hunger, we often settle for sentimental substitutes.

Dallas Willard once reflected on this confusion: "The longing for goodness and rightness makes us cling to bumper slogans and gift shop nostrums that seem deep but make no sense: 'Practice random kindness and senseless acts of beauty.'"

There may be a kernel of truth in such sayings, Willard admits, but he warns they're "180 degrees in the wrong direction" if you try to build a life on them.

Kindness, as a fruit of the Spirit, is not random or senseless. It's intentional. Cultivated. Planted and watered with care. Directed toward real people in real pain and toward broken systems in need of mending.

Willard offers a better version: "Practice routinely purposeful kindnesses and intelligent acts of beauty."

This intentionality is what the Spirit does in us and through us. Not random kindness, but patterned kindness. Not "occasional goodness," but a habit of seeking the well-being of others, even when no one is watching and even when it's not returned.

Kindness is not a slogan.
It is a way of life.
And it's the way of Jesus.

The Kindness of Jesus

If you want to understand what kindness looks like, start with Jesus.

His life was a walking, breathing revelation of divine kindness. Yes, he preached with boldness. Yes, he overturned tables in the temple. But even his anger burned with love—love for truth, love for justice, love for people held captive by sin and shame. His entire earthly ministry was soaked in compassion. His kindness was relentlessly purposeful.

He was kind to the sick.
A leper cried out: "If you are willing, you can make me clean." Jesus didn't flinch. He reached out and *touched* the untouchable. "'I am willing,' he said. 'Be clean!'" (Mark 1:40–42).

He was kind to the ashamed.
A woman caught in adultery was dragged into the public square, and her sin was used as a trap for a theological debate. Jesus kneeled beside her. He scattered her accusers with a few well-chosen words, then looked into her soul: "'Neither do I condemn you,' Jesus declared. 'Go now and leave your life of sin,'" (John 8:11).

He was kind to the invisible.
On his way to Jerusalem, he noticed a man named Zacchaeus, perched in a tree and desperate for a glimpse. Jesus didn't just *see* this man; he also invited himself into Zacchaeus's home. One act of kindness cracked open a hard heart (Luke 19:1–10).

He was kind to the grieving.
When he encountered a widow burying her only son, Jesus was moved with compassion. He walked straight into the heartbreak and raised the boy back to life (Luke 7:11–15).

He was kind to his betrayers.
At the Last Supper, he washed the feet of the very ones who would scatter, deny, and betray him. He offered bread to Judas. He looked Peter in the eye. His kindness didn't depend on the worthiness of the recipient; instead, it flowed from the fullness of his love.

He was kind even in death.
Hanging on the cross, bleeding for the sins of the world, he looked at the thief beside him and said, "Today you will be with me in paradise." He looked at the soldiers below and said, "Father, forgive them."

Kindness like Christ

This is the kindness we are called to: "Be kind and compassionate to one another, forgiving each other, just as in Christ God forgave you. Follow God's example, therefore, as dearly loved children and walk in the way of love, just as Christ loved us and gave himself up for us as a fragrant offering and sacrifice to God" (Ephesians 4:32–5:2).

Here is the motivation. We are not kind because people deserve it. We are kind because we are *dearly loved children*. We are kind because of what God has done for us in Jesus Christ. People who have love and joy and peace and patience will often be kind as a result.

So, what does kindness look like today?

You stop to listen to someone who everyone else overlooks.
You give the benefit of the doubt instead of jumping to conclusions.
You hold back a sarcastic comment and offer a blessing instead.

You send a handwritten note, not because it's efficient, but because it's meaningful.
You bring a meal to a young mom or sit in silence with someone who is grieving.
You forgive the person who didn't ask for it.
You ask your server's name and treat them with honor.
You interrupt your day to help someone get where they're going or get through what they're going through.
You speak truth in love when it would be easier to stay silent or stay angry.
You pray for someone you secretly resent.

These are not sporadic acts. They are practiced, chosen, Spirit-led acts. They are the "fragrant offerings" we give back to God, not to earn his love but because we already have it.

Kindness is not just what Jesus *did*.
It is who Jesus *was*.
And now it is who we are becoming, in him.

So, we practice by following his example.

The Fruit That Gives Away

Decades ago, I was working in middle school ministry at a church in Houston.

That summer, we took a group of students on a mission trip to a very poor part of Mexico. In a few days, we built two houses. On the last night, we gathered in small groups to process the experience. The group of girls was in tears, with each one saying it had been the best week of her life. They spoke of connection, meaning, and compassion. Meanwhile, across the way, the boys in my group looked like they were undergoing dental surgery. Their eyes were pleading with me: *Please let us go.*

I pulled one of the other leaders aside and said, "Well, the girls got it. I'm not so sure about the boys." They didn't want to sit in a circle to process or share about their feelings. They wanted to play soccer.

The next morning, we visited each of the new homes to present the families with a Spanish Bible and pray a blessing over their house. I stood at the door of the bus, counting heads, when I saw the four boys from my group walking toward me. And they were all shirtless.

I stopped them. "Fellas," I said, "you're not that built yet. The ladies are not going to be all that impressed. Put your shirts back on for the ride home."

They didn't say a word. Just pointed behind them.

There, standing by one of the new homes, was a crowd of beaming Mexican children. Each one of them was wearing an oversized, sweaty, American T-shirt. Four kids. Four shirts. Except one boy was still shirtless. One of the middle school guys leaned in and whispered, "He'd look good in your shirt, boss."

I gave him my shirt.

And I rode half-naked the long bus ride home thinking, *No, I think they got it. And, through their act of kindness, so did I.*

This is the fruit of kindness. It grows in specific soil through Spirit-led lives, in ordinary places, often in overlooked people.

It grows when we push past the slogans and bumper stickers.
It grows when we forgive, when we give, when we show up.
It grows in churches, in shelters, in auction halls, on dusty roads, and on buses full of middle school boys who are becoming more like Jesus than they even realize.

Kindness isn't always convenient.
It's rarely impressive.
But it is never wasted.

Because when the Spirit cultivates kindness in you, the world begins to taste and see what God is really like.

An Invitation for Reflection & Growth

KEY VERSE

Those who are kind benefit themselves,
but the cruel bring ruin on themselves.
—Proverbs 11:17

BIG IDEA

Kindness isn't weakness. It's intentional mercy, chosen again and again, even when it costs something. It crosses lines, disarms shame, restores dignity, and reflects the heart of a God who never gives up on us. This type of kindness can't be faked—and it won't walk away.

READING & REFLECTION

Kindness That Surprises

Read 2 Samuel 9:1–13 and Proverbs 11:17

- How does David's kindness to Mephibosheth break expectations?
- What does this act of mercy say about David's character—and about God's?

Reflection & Practice

- Where is God inviting you to show unexpected kindness?
- Look for someone who is usually overlooked. Offer them kindness that surprises them (and you). Push yourself outside your comfort zone.

Kindness That Convicts

Read Romans 2:1–4

- Why does Paul link kindness to repentance? How does that help shape your understanding of kindness?
- How might judgmental attitudes get in the way of God's mercy?

Reflection & Practice

- Where have you experienced God's kindness as the catalyst for change?
- Reflect on a time when God was kind to you, despite the fact you didn't deserve it. Let that memory soften your heart toward someone else.

Kindness That Cares

Read Luke 10:25–37

- What barriers does the Samaritan cross to care for the wounded man?
- How does Jesus define "neighbor"?

Reflection & Practice

- Where might you be called to cross a line for the sake of mercy?
- Ask God to open your eyes to a need around you—and give you the courage to move toward it.

Kindness That Endures

Read Titus 3:1–7

- What does Paul remind the church about their past—and God's mercy?
- Why is remembering our own story essential to practicing kindness?
- Where do you need God's help to keep showing kindness, even when it's hard?

Reflection & Practice

- How does God's kindness toward us reshape the way we treat others?
- Write out Titus 3:4–5, then put it somewhere where you can read it this week. Let it remind you: Kindness isn't earned. It's given. And it endures.

CULTIVATION PRACTICE: MAKE THE FIRST MOVE

Kindness rarely happens by accident. More often, it begins with a quiet, intentional decision.

This week, pause and ask yourself: *Who is God inviting me to love—especially someone I tend to overlook, avoid, or find difficult to be near?* Let the Spirit bring one name to mind. Then, respond with one tangible act of kindness—not to earn favor or fix a problem, but simply to mirror the grace you've received. Here are a few ways to begin:

- Write a note of encouragement or gratitude.
- Make a phone call, just to check in.
- Offer practical help or show up in a small but meaningful way.
- Speak a word that builds up rather than tears down.

Don't wait for the perfect moment. Don't wait for them to deserve it. Don't expect anything in return. Just *make the first move*—and let kindness do what only kindness can: soften hearts, open doors, and remind someone (maybe even you) that love still gets the final word.

A PRAYER TO CULTIVATE KINDNESS

Jesus, thank you for your kindness to me.
You moved toward me when others stepped away.
You sought me before I was ready to change.
You never treated me like a problem to fix.

I want to live that type of kindness.
Not just when it's convenient.
Not just when it makes me look good.
But when it costs me something.

When it interrupts my day.
When it means slowing down to really see someone.

Help me resist the urge to brush people off,
to judge,
to keep score.
Let your Spirit nudge me
to listen longer,
to give without expecting anything back.

I know this type of kindness doesn't come naturally.
So grow it in me.
Make it a habit, not a headline.
Let it become the shape of my life—
a reflection of your mercy and grace.

Amen.

CHAPTER 6

GOODNESS

The One Who Mends What Is Broken

As I write this, there is devastating news.

A storm had settled over the Texas Hill Country, a place that holds some of my best childhood memories. I grew up going to camp there every summer just a few miles from the town of Hunt, nestled near the Guadalupe River, where the limestone hills glow gold in the evening light and the scent of cedar hangs in the air.

But on one night, everything changed.

Rain fell hard and fast, so fast it overwhelmed the ground, the roads, the rivers. A wall of water tore through the region, washing away trees, cars, homes, lives. I saw this destructive power firsthand in 1987. I witnessed a dead cow floating down the river at what appeared to be sixty miles per hour, like it was keeping up with traffic on a highway.

The 2025 Texas Hill Country flood personally affected a family I know. My high school was extraordinarily small, and my graduating class only had twenty-one students. One of my tennis team friends had family who were too close to the overwhelming water that night. His younger brother, sister-in-law, and their two young boys had driven into the Hill Country to spend the night before picking up their daughter from camp.

All four of them were swept away in the flood. In a single night, that little girl became an orphan.

What does the goodness of God mean in a world like that?

What does it mean to speak of goodness when rivers rise and grief pours in behind them?

When we say that goodness is a fruit of the Spirit, are we talking about something sentimental?
Something naïve? Something impossible?

It is easy to believe in the goodness of God when the breeze is gentle, the food is plentiful, and the flowers are in bloom. But with eyes wide open, how do we face the harshness and heartbreak of life that makes us question whether goodness is real?

Let me clarify: The biblical word for *goodness* speaks to something deep and durable. It's about moral substance. It's about integrity that holds in the dark. In the face of evil, injustice, and devastating loss, goodness is what endures. It shows up, it acts, and it refuses to let brokenness have the final word.

Goodness is not a passive virtue, but bold evidence of God's unwavering commitment to justice, beauty, and what is right, even when, or especially when, the world is unraveling.

But how do we cling to that when life feels devastating?
What do we do with the ache behind the question: *"If God is good, then why . . . ?"*

The truth is, the fruit of the Spirit (especially goodness) isn't cultivated in controlled, comfortable environments. It doesn't grow in the greenhouse of ease.

It's forged in the storm.
It's formed in the tension between what we see and what we hope for.
It takes root when we trust God's goodness not as a feeling, but as a fact—anchored in who he is and who he says he is, not in how things appear.

What Was Meant for Harm

We're not the first to question how to make sense of a good God in a fallen world.

One of the most honest explorations of goodness in the entire Bible comes from a man whose life unraveled, again and again, through betrayal and injustice.

His name was Joseph.

He was betrayed by his brothers. Thrown into a pit. Sold into slavery. Falsely accused. Imprisoned and forgotten. Years of silence. Years of waiting.

But eventually, through a strange and winding path, Joseph rose to power in Egypt. A famine struck the land, and his brothers—the very ones who had betrayed him—came to him, desperate for food. They didn't recognize him at first. But when they did, they feared he'd retaliate.

Instead, Joseph said, "You intended to harm me, but God intended it for good to accomplish what is now being done, the saving of many lives" (Genesis 50:20).

It's one of the boldest declarations of faith in all of Scripture.

Not a dismissal of the pain. Not a pious silver lining. But a reckoning: *Even in the place where I was wounded, God was working.*

The Hebrew word for "good"—*tov*—is the same word used in Genesis 1 when God looked over creation and called it very good. But here, Joseph uses it to name something that came out of betrayal.

Tov, in this moment, is not untouched innocence. It is goodness forged in the fire of suffering.

The goodness of God doesn't deny that evil happens. Instead, it declares that evil doesn't get to win.

A Different Kind of Knowledge

This is the kind of goodness the Spirit cultivates in us—not the kind that simply knows what is good, but the kind that becomes good through faithful presence, even in pain.

Harvard professor and psychiatrist Robert Coles once wrote an article titled "The Disparity Between Intellect and Character." In it, he reflected on the gap between what people know and how they live—what he called "the daunting task of connecting intellect to character."

The article grew out of a conversation he'd had with a young woman from a working-class background in the Midwest. She was a student at Harvard, cleaning dorm rooms to pay her way through school, the very rooms that belonged to students she sat beside in philosophy and ethics classes.

She told Coles that many of her classmates, some of the brightest and most praised for their moral reasoning, treated her with coldness, condescension, and sometimes crude disrespect.

One, a star student in their moral philosophy class, repeatedly propositioned her for sex.

Eventually, she couldn't take it anymore. She left her job. She left school. And before she left, she had one final conversation with Coles: "I've been taking all these philosophy courses, and we talk about what's true, what's important, what's good. Well, how do you teach people to be good? What's the point of knowing good if you don't keep trying to become a good person?"

That's the question this chapter is trying to answer.

Goodness isn't proven by how well you can argue about and articulate it. It's proven by whether or not someone feels the presence of God's kindness, justice, and love through you.

Joseph didn't just speak about goodness. He embodied it. Not because he had the right answers, but because he trusted God with his pain—and allowed that trust to transform his actions.

The fruit of the Spirit is goodness.

The question is not just "Can you write an essay on what is good?" It's "Are you becoming someone through whom God's goodness flows?"

What Is Goodness?

But what exactly is *goodness*—and how is it different from love, joy, peace, patience, or kindness?

It's a fair question. Goodness can seem like the umbrella under which all the other fruit live. After all, isn't love good? Isn't kindness good? Isn't joy good?

Yes, but goodness, in the biblical sense, is not just a blend of virtues. It's a distinct fruit because it reflects something specific: *integrity.*

If love is the motive and kindness is the method, goodness is the *moral fiber* that runs through it all. It's the alignment between conviction and action, between what you believe and how you live. It's what happens when qualities like *truth* and *love* take a walk together.

Paul lists goodness alongside these other virtues not as a generic stand-in, but as a powerful marker of *strong character*. It means doing what is right even when it costs you. It means having both a spine and a heart. It means refusing to settle for sentiment or cynicism, and instead cultivating a life that reflects the wholeness, justice, and righteousness of God.

In a world of compromise and performance, *goodness is integrity in motion.*

And we see it in Scripture.

Goodness is Boaz, quietly protecting Ruth's dignity when she was vulnerable, going above the letter of the law to honor her with compassion and strength.

Goodness is the Good Samaritan, crossing cultural boundaries to care for a wounded man who had been left for dead. He doesn't just feel pity, he *acts*. He interrupts his day, gives his money, and uses his influence to restore someone else's life.

Goodness is Daniel, refusing to bend to corrupt power while still living and working with excellence. His character isn't defined by outrage, but by resolve.

Goodness is John the Baptist, confronting corruption not with violence or vengeance, but with truth and integrity, even when it costs him his life.

And goodness still shows up today.

It's the business leader who walks away from a profitable deal because it cuts ethical corners. The nurse who treats the difficult patient with tenderness. The teenager who befriends the classmate everyone else ignores. The foster parent who holds steady in the mess of someone else's trauma. The friend who refuses to gossip, even when it's juicy.

Goodness is rarely flashy. It usually happens offstage. It does the right thing, at the right time, in the right way, for the right reasons.

It's not always praised. But it is always powerful.

Surely Goodness

If you've ever been to a funeral, you've probably heard Psalm 23.

It's the psalm that comforts the grieving and anchors the anxious. It speaks of green pastures and still waters, valleys and shadows, tables and oil. But the line that stops me every time is the last one: "Surely goodness and mercy shall follow me all the days of my life, and I shall dwell in the house of the Lord forever" (Psalm 23:6 ESV).

Goodness and mercy.

In Hebrew, the word translated "follow" is actually stronger than it sounds. It's not a casual trailing behind. It's a pursuit. A chasing down. The same verb is used elsewhere in the Old Testament for armies pursuing their enemies.

Which means this: God's goodness chases you.

It doesn't just tag along for the ride. It goes after you.

Even in the valley and even in the dark. Even in the moments when you aren't sure you believe any of this anymore.

God's goodness is not merely a quality. It's a reality. It's not merely a feeling. It's a pursuit. It's what searches for misplaced coins and lost sheep and wayward sons (Luke 15). It's not confined to the gentle or sentimental. It has grit. It has staying power. It moves with intention.

Yes, God is loving. Yes, God is merciful. But there is a unique weight to his goodness—a wholeness, a rightness, a holiness in motion.

Goodness is what restores what was lost. What makes wrong things right. What refuses to leave you where you are.

It's what Joseph trusted. It's what the psalmist declares. It's what a girl in the Hill Country flood still needs to know is true.

And it's the reminder we need too.

Goodness in the Basement

God's goodness is not an abstract concept. It has hands and feet. It walks into flooded streets and church basements. It shows up through people who say yes to love when it's costly and inconvenient.

I saw that firsthand after another flood, this one hundreds of miles east of the Texas Hill Country.

It was 2005. Hurricane Katrina had devastated New Orleans. Thousands were displaced overnight. Buses filled with evacuees fanned out across the country, and many were brought to where we lived in San Antonio.

Our church was asked to activate an emergency shelter, not for the general population, but for people with medical conditions who couldn't be housed in larger group settings. We said yes.

Within hours, our classrooms were transformed into living quarters. Church members signed up for overnight shifts. Nurses took vacation time to be present. People cooked, cleaned, prayed, cried, and listened.

For weeks, our building never slept. And neither did God's goodness.

Meanwhile, in our youth group, a student going through confirmation was wrestling with serious doubts. She was thoughtful and empathetic, and also very skeptical. Her barrier to faith wasn't personal suffering; it was global suffering. She couldn't reconcile a good God with the pain she saw in the world.

And she made that very clear. She wasn't angry for herself. She was angry on behalf of others.

But then, something changed.

The youth group volunteered at the shelter. This student came face-to-face with the very suffering she had used as an argument against God. But more importantly, she came close with a church full of ordinary people responding to that suffering with extraordinary love. She saw compassion in action. She saw the light shining in the basement of a church during one of the darkest times in modern American history.

And the darkness didn't win.

Her doubts didn't evaporate overnight. But they started to bend under the mass of something undeniable: *goodness*. Real, embodied, Spirit-fueled goodness.

She later told me that the shelter experience was the moment her perspective shifted. She realized that the presence of suffering wasn't proof of God's absence—it was the very place God often shows up through his people.

"For we are God's handiwork," Paul writes in Ephesians 2:10, "created in Christ Jesus to do good works, which God prepared in advance for us to do."

Jesus said it another way: "Let your light shine before others, that they may see your good deeds and glorify your Father in heaven" (Matthew 5:16).

Sometimes, people come to believe in God not because of a sermon, but because someone made them dinner. Not because of a theological argument, but because someone changed their bandages. Not because evil disappeared, but because they saw goodness refuse to leave.

That's what the fruit of the Spirit does.
It shines.
It serves.
It stays.

Surely goodness and mercy shall pursue us—even into the storm. And sometimes, goodness looks a lot like a teenager watching a church become the hands and feet of Jesus.

Goodness That Holds and Moves

So what do we do with all of this?

We live in a world where floods still rise. Where families still grieve. Where suffering still raises its fist and demands answers.

And yet God's goodness still pursues. It meets us in the pit like Joseph. It walks with us through the valley like David. It shows up in church basements and broken hearts, in acts of mercy, sacrifice, and service.

That's why Paul could write these words to the early church, not from a place of ease, but from the middle of hardship: "And we know that in all things God works for the good of those who love him, who have been called according to his purpose" (Romans 8:28).

That verse has been misused, oversimplified, even weaponized at times. But when it's read slowly and truthfully, it is not a promise that everything is good—it's a promise that nothing is beyond God's power to redeem. It's a promise that even in the wreckage, God is still at work.

And that his goodness still has the final word.

But it's not just a comfort. It's a calling.

Because while we rest in the assurance that God is working for good, we are also invited to walk in that goodness: "He has shown you, O mortal, what is good. And what does the LORD require of you? To act justly and to love mercy and to walk humbly with your God" (Micah 6:8).

This is goodness in motion. Justice pursued. Mercy embraced. Humility chosen.

So how do we reconnect with the goodness of God?

Start with gratitude. Make a list. Give thanks. Look for beauty—especially in the unexpected places. Take note of people who radiate kindness and wholeness and move toward them. Serve someone who cannot pay you back. Forgive someone. Forgive yourself. Pray Psalm 23 slowly. Read the Gospels and watch how Jesus walks.

But don't do it alone.

Years ago, I took my first trip to Africa. I was stunned by the depth of poverty and the harshness of life in some of the villages we visited. But what struck me even more deeply was the joy. The resilience. The community. And most of all, the refrain.

Every time two people greeted each other, it began with a call and response:
"God is good."
"All the time."
"And all the time."
"God is good."

It wasn't cliché. It was conviction. It was a declaration that God's goodness was more durable than despair.

Jesus once said, "No one is good but God alone." That truth humbles us. But it also gives us hope. Because in Jesus Christ, God has shared his goodness with us. He has come to restore what was broken, to heal what was lost, to make us right with him and one another.

We need to let the world see not just what we believe, but the goodness of the One who is still cultivating that belief into action.

Let your light shine.
Let goodness grow.
Let the Spirit move through you.

Because the world doesn't just need people who can explain what's good. It needs people who embody it. It needs the church, and it needs you.

An Invitation for Reflection & Growth

KEY VERSE

To do what is right and just
is more acceptable to the LORD than sacrifice.
—Proverbs 21:3

BIG IDEA

Goodness isn't just about being nice; it's about doing what is right. It shines with integrity in a world of compromise. It forgives when it could retaliate. It speaks truth with grace and seeks healing over harm. True goodness flows from a God who is just and kind, a God who is making all things new.

READING & REFLECTION

Goodness That Works

Read Ephesians 2:1–10 and Proverbs 21:3

- What does it mean to be "created in Christ Jesus to do good works"?
- How does goodness flow from grace instead of guilt?

Reflection & Practice

- Describe a time when you felt invited to do good for someone.
- Take a moment to reflect on a good work you've *witnessed*—not something you did, but something you had the privilege to see. Perhaps like John Ortberg, you were able to watch someone else bless goodness on another. How did that moment witness in your life?

Goodness That Gives

Read Mark 10:17–31

- Why does Jesus challenge the rich man's understanding of "good"?
- What does this story teach about surrender and the good life?

Reflection & Practice

- Where is God inviting you to let go in order to follow him?

- Ask yourself, *What am I clinging to that's keeping me from something better?* When you receive your answer, pray for courage to release it.

Goodness That Reconciles

Read Genesis 50:15–21

- What stands out to you in Joseph's response to his brothers?
- How does goodness rewrite a story of pain into one of purpose?

Reflection & Practice

- Where might God be calling you to choose forgiveness over bitterness?
- Write down a hurt you've been carrying and ask God to help you begin rewriting it with grace.

Goodness That Overcomes

Read Romans 12:17–21

- How does Paul describe the way Christians should respond to evil?
- What does it mean to "overcome evil with good"?

Reflection & Practice

- Where do you need to resist retaliation and respond with mercy?
- Think of someone who has wronged you. Pray for them today—not as an enemy, but as someone Jesus loves.

CULTIVATION PRACTICE: RETURN THE GOOD

Goodness is more than a virtue—it's a way of joining God in the healing of the world. This week, take time to reflect on the goodness that flows in and through your life. Use these three prompts to guide you:

1. **Received Goodness**
   What is one good thing someone has done for you recently?
   Pause to name it. Praise God for receiving goodness in the world.

2. **Transforming Goodness**
   Where do you sense God doing something good within you right now?
   It may be slow or hidden—but name it with hope.

3. **Shared Goodness**
   What is one good thing you can do for someone else this week—especially someone who may not be expecting it?

Write your responses on three separate cards, sticky notes, or journal entries. Keep them somewhere visible. And then—*act on at least one of them.* Because goodness isn't meant to stay inside us. It's meant to *move,* to *bless,* to *mend what's been broken*—starting with the small spaces where we live and love.

A PRAYER TO CULTIVATE GOODNESS

God, I want to believe you are good—
not just when life is beautiful,
but when things are falling apart.
When prayers go unanswered,
when grief hits close to home,
when I'm not sure what to do with my pain.

Help me hold on to your goodness in those moments.

Not as a feeling I have to chase,
but as a truth I can stand on.

You've shown me again and again
that your goodness is not sentimental—
it's steady.
It shows up.
It stays.

Grow that kind of goodness in me.
The kind that holds fast under pressure.
The kind that moves toward the pain.

Teach me to live in a way that reflects your heart—
to act justly,
to love mercy,
to walk humbly.
To bring healing where there's been harm.
Hope where there's been despair.
Light where it still feels dark.

Thank you for pursuing me with your goodness—
even when I've doubted,
even when I've run.
Shape my life to look more like yours.

Amen.

INTERLUDE

URBAN RECIPE

A few years ago, I attended a food co-op gathering hosted by Urban Recipe—a remarkable organization in Atlanta committed to long-term food security. I wasn't there to speak or lead. I just went with a handful of people from our church to learn.

At first glance, it looked like what you might expect: a parking lot, a truck, boxes of produce, people moving briskly from station to station. But pretty quickly, I realized something was different.

This wasn't a handout. It was a harvest, meant to be shared and stewarded by everyone present.

Instead of waiting in line for a bag of groceries to be handed to them, members of the co-op were working together to unload the truck, sort the food, and pack boxes—not just for themselves, but for one another. There was joyous laughter and sweat earned by hard work.

There were familiar greetings and inside jokes. This wasn't a moment of charity; it was a community.

And I started to understand the deeper difference.

In a typical food pantry, you show up with need and leave with provision. And thank God for that. Sometimes that's exactly what's required—emergency assistance, no strings attached. But a co-op is something else entirely. You don't just receive. You contribute, come early, and stay late. You carry your box—and someone else's. You offer what you have. You receive what you need. And in the process, something grows.

Urban Recipe calls it "food security." But it felt like more than that. It felt like cultivation.

Because cultivation is always communal.

You can't do it alone—not really. You might till your own soil. You might plant your own seeds. But fruitfulness, in the truest sense, is something we share.

The fruit of the Spirit was never meant to grow in isolation. Love needs someone to embrace. Joy needs someone to sing with. Peace needs someone to speak to. Patience needs someone to wait for. Kindness, goodness, faithfulness, gentleness, and self-control—all of them come alive in relationship.

And this is what I've learned as a pastor: One of the greatest enemies of spiritual transformation is not a lack of willpower. It's isolation.

Most people want to grow. They just don't know how to begin or how to keep going when it gets hard. But something powerful happens when you move from "You should help" to "Come with me."

There's a world of difference between a general appeal from the stage and a personal invitation from the floor. Growth accelerates when people are invited to serve, to risk, to show up in communities that are big enough to dare and small enough to care.

That's what Paul was getting at in Galatians 6, just after his famous list. He didn't end the chapter with a warm benediction. He gave a command: "Carry each other's burdens, and in this way you will fulfill the law of Christ" (Galatians 6:2).

Notice, he doesn't say to admire one another's fruit. He says to carry one another's burdens. Because the garden of the Spirit doesn't grow well in solitude. It grows best in shared soil.

It grows when we bear with the difficult people.
It grows when we celebrate someone else's harvest.
It grows when we confess, forgive, pray, grieve, laugh, and endure—together.

Community doesn't just happen. It must be cultivated. And not in perfect conditions. Real community is forged in the tension of unmet expectations, delayed apologies, awkward moments, and imperfect people who choose to show up again.

Just like that co-op.
Just like the church is when she's at her best.

Maybe this is the Spirit's invitation for us today, not just to bear fruit, but to bear it together.
To bring what we have.
To receive what we need.
To stay long enough to become more than consumers.
To join the long, faithful work of helping one another flourish.

Because in the garden of the Spirit, we grow best with one another.

CHAPTER 7

FAITHFULNESS

The One Who Keeps His Promises

Several years ago, a toy company started selling a new action figure in Great Britain. The toy was called "Invisible Jim." It wasn't expensive, only about three US dollars, but it was flying off the shelves like mad. The packaging looked thrilling, making all kinds of outrageous boasts: "Not seen on TV!" "Camouflage sold separately!" "Equipped with special X-ray vision!" It sounded like the kind of toy every boy would beg to have.

But here's the catch: *There was no Jim.* Nothing was inside the box. The whole product was literally just packaging. When the first shipments arrived, distributors called the manufacturer, assuming it was a colossal mistake. But no—this was the actual product. Great marketing. Great packaging. Empty box.

It was a joke product, of course, but it hit a little too close to home.

Have you ever felt like some promises are just too good to be true?
A politician promising to make your life better.
A boss guaranteeing benefits that quietly disappear in the fine print.
A preacher offering peace or prosperity if you just have enough faith.
A friend declaring they will be there but never showing up.

It's not hard to understand why people get skeptical. Especially when it comes to religion. For many, it feels like all hype—great promises, glossy words, beautiful packaging . . . but nothing inside the box.

Faithfulness is what makes the difference. It's what turns a promise into something real.

The late psychologist Lewis Smedes once wrote, "Everything in human history depends on a promise made and a promise kept."

He's right. Every marriage begins with a promise made and depends on it being kept. Every parent-child relationship is built on trust, on spoken and unspoken promises. Every friendship, every neighborhood, every nation, every church community stands or falls on this question: *Will we be faithful?*

Without faithfulness, the world falls apart.
With it, we hold together.

And that's where we need to begin. Because in a world of broken promises, God is the one who keeps his word.

Promise After Promise

At the very heart of our faith is *promise*. Christianity begins and ends with covenant. From the first pages to the last, the Bible is a diary of God's faithfulness to what he has said.

He promised Adam that he would provide.
He promised Noah that he would remember.
He promised Abraham that he would lead.
He promised Jacob that he would go with him.
He promised Moses and the Israelites that he would deliver them.

Over and over again, God speaks and then acts. He does not forget. He does not flinch. He does not fail.

A student of Scripture once spent a year and a half combing through the entire Bible to count each individual promise. The final tally? *7,487 promises from God to humanity.*

Let that sink in for a moment. God didn't make just one or two sweeping declarations. He filled the story with promise after promise—each one revealing his character, his heart, and his faithfulness.

It's worth a flyover view of the whole Bible. He promised . . .

. . . Noah that he would never again destroy the earth.
. . . Abraham that he would guide us by faith.
. . . Sarah a child in her old age.
. . . Jacob that he would never leave him.
. . . Joseph that what others meant for harm, God would use for good.

. . . The Hebrew midwives, Shiphrah and Puah, that no earthly tyrant is greater than God.

. . . Moses that he would make a way through the sea.

. . . Joshua that God would fight for his people.

. . . Gideon that victory would come through weakness.

. . . Ruth that love is stronger than bitterness.

. . . Samuel that the voice of God still speaks.

. . . David that his kingdom would never end.

. . . Solomon wisdom for the asking.

. . . Elijah that he was not alone.

. . . Elisha that resurrection was real.

. . . Isaiah that those who wait on the Lord will renew their strength.

. . . Jeremiah that God's Word would be written on our hearts.

. . . Ezekiel that dry bones can live again.

. . . Amos that justice will roll down like waters and righteousness like a never-ending stream.

. . . Malachi that you can't out-give God.

. . . Zephaniah that we will have a home.

. . . Mary that the Promised One would be born in her.

. . . A Samaritan woman that living water never runs dry.

. . . A paralyzed man that he would walk again.

. . . A bleeding woman that she was his daughter.

. . . Peter that he would become a fisher of people.

. . . Paul that grace is sufficient and power is perfected in weakness.

. . . John that God will wipe away every tear from our eyes. No more death. No more disease. No more pain. Behold—God is making all things new.

This is the record of our faith: promise after promise, made and kept. This is what faithfulness looks like.

Hidden in Plain Sight

A few months ago, Japan made international news for something rather surprising. It turns out they had miscounted their own islands.

For decades, Japan officially listed 6,852 islands within its territory. That number appeared in textbooks, on maps, and in government reports. But recently, the Geospatial Information Authority of Japan conducted a far more accurate digital survey using advanced mapping technology. When the data came back, it revealed something stunning: *There weren't 6,852 islands. There were 14,125.*

They had missed more than *seven thousand islands*—not because the islands weren't there, but because the tools they used before weren't precise enough to see them all. Most of these islands had always existed. They had just gone uncounted. Hidden in plain sight.

It wasn't that Japan suddenly got bigger overnight.
It's that they had *far more* islands than they realized.

When I read that, I thought: *That's exactly how it is with the promises of God.*

Most people, if asked, could probably name a handful of promises they can recall, maybe ten or twelve. The promise of heaven. The promise of forgiveness. The promise that God loves you. That's what shows up in our mental maps.

But the truth is, *there are thousands more.*

They're there in the text. There in the story. There in your life.

And like those unmapped islands, they've been quietly shaping the coastline of faith the whole time—whether we noticed them or not.

God's promises are not rare. They are not small. They are not wishful thinking. They are real. They are rich. They are waiting to be discovered.

The more closely you look at Scripture, the more clearly you begin to see them. Promises for the weary. Promises for the bold, the lost, the grieving, the wandering, the hopeful, the faithful, the fearful. Promises in every chapter, every season, every page.

We don't need new promises. We just need better eyes. Because what we thought was a scattered handful is actually a vast and abundant inheritance.

You're not standing on a bare and barren spiritual coastline.
You're standing on the edge of a land filled with promise.
You just might have underestimated what's already yours.

The Covenant Path

Of all the promises God has made, perhaps none is more foundational than the one he made to Abraham.

Back in Genesis 12, God makes the first move: "Go . . . to the land I will show you. . . . And I will bless you; I will make your name great, . . . and all peoples on earth will be blessed through you" (Genesis 12:1–3). That was the call and the beginning of the promise.

Then, in Genesis 15, the conversation continues. Abraham is older now. The promise of a child still unfulfilled. The land still a dream. And Abraham is wrestling with questions we all ask at some point: *Can I really trust what God has said? Will he actually come through?*

That's when God pulls Abraham out of his tent and says, "Look up at the sky and count the stars—if indeed you can count them." Then he whispers: "So shall your offspring be."

And in that moment, Abraham doesn't just nod politely—he believes. The Scripture says, "Abram believed the LORD, and he credited it to him as righteousness" (Genesis 15:6).

What happens next is one of the strangest and most powerful scenes in all the Bible.

It's an ancient text, so it requires a little explanation. God tells Abraham to bring him animals—a cow, a goat, a ram, a dove, and a pigeon. Abraham doesn't even ask what they're for; he already knows. In that culture, this was covenant language. You didn't "make" a covenant. You *cut* one. Literally.

The animals are cut in half. The bloody halves are arranged in two rows, forming a kind of pathway. This was the ancient way of sealing a deal. Both parties would walk between the pieces as if to say, "If I break my word, may I become like these animals." The covenant walk was serious business. Not symbolic. Sacrificial. You didn't walk lightly through blood.

But here's the twist.

As night comes, Abraham falls into a deep, fearful sleep. And in that darkness, something stunning happens. A smoking firepot and a blazing torch—symbols of God's presence—appear and pass between the pieces alone (Genesis 15:17).

God walks the covenant path by himself.

Abraham never takes a step.

In other words, God is saying: "This promise does not depend on you. It depends on me. I will keep my word even if it costs me everything." And that's exactly what happens.

Because when the covenant was broken (and it *was* broken), God didn't void the agreement. He didn't walk away. He walked toward the cross.

Jesus, on the night he was betrayed, held up the cup and said, "This cup is the new covenant in my blood" (Luke 22:20).

It was as if he were saying, "You've broken the promise. But I will pay the price. I will walk the blood path. I will be torn so that you can be restored."

This is the breathtaking faithfulness of God. Not just making promises but keeping them. Not just inviting us into covenant but carrying the cost when we can't and don't.

And there's more.

Later, in Genesis 17, God changes Abram's name to Abraham. Sarai becomes Sarah. It seems small, just one added letter. But in Hebrew, that *h* letter is *hei*, the sound of breath. God puts his breath into their very names, just as he breathed into Adam, and eventually will breathe into the Upper Room after Easter. What was dead now has life. What was barren now bears fruit.

That's what God's faithfulness does.
It doesn't merely promise life.
It makes you alive.

Becoming Faithful People

So what does all of this mean for us?

If faithfulness is at the very heart of who God is—if he is the one who walks the path alone, who keeps his word no matter the cost—then what does it mean to be people of faithfulness in a world of flakes, fakes, and fine print?

We don't live in a *covenant* culture. We live in a *cancel* culture.

In today's world, commitment is often optional. Promises are provisional. Words are flexible. If it's inconvenient, we bail. If it's uncomfortable, we ghost. If it's costly, we rewrite the terms. Marriage vows, church membership, job loyalty, even everyday friendships—we keep our options open. And in doing so, we often miss out on the deeper life that only grows over time: the fruit of faithfulness.

But here's the good news: *The Spirit can grow this in us.*

Galatians 5 doesn't say, "Try harder to be faithful." It says, "The fruit of the Spirit is . . . faithfulness."

In other words, this isn't just about grinding out promises or white-knuckling your commitments. It's about staying rooted in the God who is always faithful and letting his Spirit shape your character to look like his.

Faithfulness shows up not just in heroic moments, but in everyday ones.
It looks like keeping your word when no one would notice if you didn't.
Showing up to the hard conversation instead of avoiding it.
Doing what you said you'd do even when the feeling has faded.
Loving the person who isn't easy to love today.
Staying in the story God has written, even when it's not the one you expected.

Faithfulness is long obedience in the same direction. It's the teacher who shows up every morning for students who rarely say thank you. The caregiver who keeps serving when there's no applause. The friend who doesn't walk away just because it's awkward or painful. The spouse who stays, prays, and keeps believing even through the dry seasons.

And here's the miracle: When you let God grow this fruit in your life, it doesn't just bless *you*—it blesses *others*. Your faithfulness becomes someone else's shelter. Someone else's hope. Someone else's glimpse of what God is like.

Because when people see you keep a promise, they start to believe again that maybe God keeps his too.

So let's be the kind of people who reflect the One who keeps covenant.

Let's be the kind of people whose "yes" means yes, whose presence can be counted on, whose love stays rooted even when storms come.

Jesus put it this way in the Sermon on the Mount: "All you need to say is simply 'Yes' or 'No'; anything beyond this comes from the evil one" (Matthew 5:37).

He was teaching that people who live in God's kingdom shouldn't need to prop up their words with elaborate oaths or dramatic guarantees. You don't have to say, "I swear to God," or "I promise on my life." You simply say "yes" and live like you mean it. Or you say "no" and stand by it with grace.

Because when the Spirit of faithfulness is growing in you, your word begins to carry weight. Not because you shout it louder, but because you live it deeper.

You become the kind of person others don't have to double-check.
The kind of friend who can be counted on.
The kind of leader whose consistency is more powerful than charisma.
The kind of worker who isn't cutting corners.
The kind of disciple whose quiet *yes* echoes the faithfulness of Jesus himself.

Let's be faithful. Not perfectly, but persistently. Not in our own strength, but through the Spirit who breathes life into dry bones and barren hearts.

Because "the one who calls you is faithful, and he will do it" (1 Thessalonians 5:24).

Marked by the Promise

The great characters of the Bible are not great because of what they did. They are great because they were *bearers of the promise.*

If you read Scripture and keep thinking the people in it are heroes, you're missing the point. They were ordinary men and women—flawed, fearful, fragile. Just like us. What set them apart wasn't their strength but their *trust.* They carried the promises of God like a flame in the dark, often stumbling, but never letting it go out.

This is what I want my life to be. Not showy. Not perfect. But *faithful.* A life with the fingerprints of God's promise all over it.

A good friend of my congregation, and my mentor, Vic Pentz, once told a story I'll never forget.

A long time ago, Vic bought a navy blazer at Nordstrom. At first, it seemed like a good purchase. But the more he wore it, the more he realized he didn't like it. The color was off. It attracted lint like a magnet. After wearing the blazer for a while, he stuffed it in the back of his closet and forgot about it.

All the while, there was this little thought in the back of his mind: *Nordstrom has that famous unconditional return policy.* But he kept telling himself it was too late. He'd had it too long. Worn it too much. No way they'd take it back.

Finally, one day, he decided to try. What did he have to lose?

He pulled the blazer out, made sure it looked extra bad, and took it back to the store. He walked in feeling nervous, like he was trying to pull off a con. He rehearsed his speech: "I've had this blazer for over a year. I've worn it a lot. It's the wrong color. It attracts lint. I'd like to return it."

He stood there, waiting for the salesman to object.

Instead, the man with a handlebar mustache just shook his head and said, "For heaven's sake, what took you so long? Let's go find you a blazer."

Ten minutes later, Vic walked out with a new blazer—one that was more expensive than the original. And it didn't cost him a dime.

Now, hear me: This isn't a pitch about quality retail. This is a story about *faithfulness*. About promise.

I imagine there are some reading this who've heard God's promise again and again—maybe since childhood. But for whatever reason, you've never really *trusted* it. Never tested it. Never activated it. You leave it hanging like an unused jacket in the closet of your soul. You assume it's too late. Too worn. Too good to be true.

Or maybe others of you have confused promise with *performance*. You wake up every day with your value meter at zero, and you climb back on the treadmill to prove yourself—to God, to others, even to yourself. But deep down, you know you'll never be good enough. The chase never ends.

Some of you ignore the promise, assuming it couldn't possibly apply to you.

Others try to earn the promise, assuming it depends on you.

Too good to be true. Or never good enough.

But no matter where you fall on that spectrum, I believe God is here, smiling, shaking his head with mercy, and saying, *"For heaven's sake, what took you so long?"*

God both makes the promise and keeps the promise.

He is the One who cut the covenant and walked through the blood path alone.
The One who said, "I will pay."
The One who stretched out his arms on a cross, not as a victim but as a willing Savior.
The One whose last will and testament, sealed in his blood, can't be altered, improved, or undone.

You don't need to negotiate it.
You don't need to make it.
All you can do is *rely on it.*

And let your life be marked—deeply, joyfully, unmistakably—by the faithfulness of God.

Let your *yes* be yes.
Let your word carry weight.
Let your roots go deep.
Let the Spirit grow fruit in you that reflects the One who never fails.

Because "the one who calls you is faithful,
and he will do it" (1 Thessalonians 5:24).

An Invitation for Reflection & Growth

KEY VERSE

Let love and faithfulness never leave you;
bind them around your neck,
write them on the tablet of your heart.
Then you will win favor and a good name
in the sight of God and man.
—Proverbs 3:3–4

BIG IDEA

Faithfulness is staying true to your word, your people, and your God, even when it's hard. It doesn't waver with moods or seasons. It shows up, stands firm, and finishes well. In a world of shallow commitments and broken trust, faithfulness points to the God who always keeps his promises.

READING & REFLECTION

Faithfulness That Draws Near

Read Hebrews 10:19–25 and Proverbs 3:3–4

- What rhythms of faithfulness are named in this passage?
- How does drawing near to God shape your faithfulness to others?

Reflection & Practice

- Where are you tempted to drift—and what helps you hold fast?
- Circle one phrase from these passages you just read to carry with you. Let it be your daily anchor.

Faithfulness That Risks

Read Matthew 25:14–30

- What do the faithful servants do differently from the one who buries his talent?
- What risks might faithfulness require in your life?

Reflection & Practice

- Where is God calling you to act rather than avoid?
- Name a gift or opportunity you've been sitting on. Take one small step to invest it.

Faithfulness That Provides

Read 1 Kings 17:1–16

- How does God provide for Elijah, the widow, and her son?
- What does this story teach you about daily trust?

Reflection & Practice

- Where do you need to lean into God's faithfulness today?
- Each morning this week, pray: "Give us this day our daily bread." Watch how God provides.

Faithfulness That Stands Firm

Read Daniel 3

- How do Shadrach, Meshach, and Abednego show courage?

- What makes their faithfulness so powerful, even if God hadn't saved them?

Reflection & Practice

- Where are you called to stand for truth, even if the outcome is uncertain?
- Write a declaration of trust that begins with *"Even if not . . ."* and let it become your anthem of faithfulness even in the face of uncertainty.

Faithfulness That Finishes Well

Read 2 Timothy 4:6–8

- How does Paul reflect on his life and ministry?
- What does it look like to run the race with faithfulness?

Reflection & Practice

- Where do you want to finish well, and what needs tending now to make that possible?
- Think of someone who has finished their race well. What habits or patterns can you learn from their example?

CULTIVATION PRACTICE: MARK THE MILESTONES

Faithfulness isn't just about crossing the finish line; it's about walking with God every step of the way. This week, draw a winding path across a blank page. Along that path, mark three sacred moments:

- A place where you nearly gave up—but didn't.
- A place where God carried you when you couldn't move forward on your own.

- A place where someone spoke life into you and helped you keep going.

Sit with the path you've drawn. Thank God for the grace in each mile behind you, and ask for the courage to trust him with the road still ahead.

A PRAYER TO CULTIVATE FAITHFULNESS

God, you keep your promises.
Even when I forget.
Even when I doubt.
Even when I walk away.

You are steady when everything else shifts.
You don't ignore or bail or change your mind.
You are faithful—through storm and silence,
through joy and failure,
through every long stretch where I wonder if you're still near.

Grow in me the kind of faithfulness
that shows up without needing recognition,
that keeps going when the excitement fades,
that honors small commitments
as holy ground.

Let my "yes" be real.
Let my presence matter.
Let my words carry the weight of your love.
Make me a person someone can count on—
not because I'm strong,
but because you are.

Thank you for carrying the covenant
when I couldn't.
For walking the path alone
so I could walk with you.

Shape me with your Spirit.
Steady me with your grace.
Make me faithful like you.

Amen.

CHAPTER 8

GENTLENESS

The One Who Speaks Tenderly

How many words do you think you speak in a single day?

Researchers have studied this question, and while the exact number varies from person to person, studies suggest that the average American adult speaks around sixteen thousand words each day. Over the course of a lifetime, that adds up to nearly half a billion words.

To put that in perspective: If you were to read the entire Bible out loud (cover to cover), you could do so 625 times and still not use up all the words you're likely to speak in your life.

That's an extraordinary amount of speech. And it raises an important question: What are we doing with all those words?

In church, we often talk about what we believe. We talk about how we think and how we act. But we don't always talk about how we speak—not just the content of our words, but the tone, timing, and spirit in which they are spoken.

Scripture tells us that words carry power. Proverbs 18:21 puts it starkly: "The tongue has the power of life and death." Our words can build up or tear down. They can bless or belittle. They can create trust or destroy it. Sometimes a word of encouragement stays with a person for a lifetime. Sometimes a single careless sentence leaves a wound that doesn't heal.

It's striking that when we open the Bible to its very first page, we find that the first thing God does is speak. Genesis 1 describes a rhythmic cadence of divine speech: "Let there be light," "Let there be sky," "Let the land produce." God's words are not empty—they are creative. What he says comes into being.

The Jesus Storybook Bible, in its poetic retelling of Genesis, imagines God's creation as a kind of gentle greeting: "Hello, light. Hello, sky. Hello, sea. You're good. You're very good." It envisions creation not as a command shouted from above, but as the beginning of a conversation spoken face-to-face. In this telling, the first thing Adam and Eve see is the face of God, and the first thing they hear is his voice.

Even more remarkable is that God doesn't stop speaking after creation. He invites humanity to join the conversation. In the garden, God brings the animals to Adam and asks him to name them. God, who spoke the universe into existence, now shares the creative work with us. He entrusts us with words—not just as tools of expression, but as instruments of care, relationship, and stewardship.

This is where gentleness enters the picture. Gentleness is often misunderstood as weakness. But in Scripture, gentleness is a mark of wisdom and strength—strength that is restrained and used for good. Gentleness is the Spirit's way of shaping how we speak. It is not just what we say that matters, but how we say it.

In a world that rewards volume, outrage, and force, gentleness is a rare and powerful fruit. It reflects the character of the One who is "gentle and lowly in heart" (Matthew 11:29 ESV), who speaks not to dominate but to heal, not to condemn but to invite.

Gentleness is how God speaks to us. And it is how God longs to speak through us.

The Very Heart of God

It is no small thing to say that God speaks gently. But it becomes even more astounding when we consider how Jesus describes himself.

Across the four Gospels, there are eighty-nine chapters filled with the words and actions of Jesus—miracles, parables, sermons, confrontations, prayers. But in all those chapters, there is only one place where Jesus opens a window into his own heart. Only one moment when he tells us what he is like at the core.

In Matthew 11:28–29, Jesus says, "Come to me, all you who are weary and burdened, and I will give you rest. Take my yoke upon you and learn from me, for I am *gentle and humble in heart*, and you will find rest for your souls" (emphasis mine).

Not powerful and commanding. Not brilliant and strategic. Not passionate and pure—though he is all those things.

But gentle. And lowly.

Dane Ortlund, in his book by the title *Gentle and Lowly*, writes, "In the one place in the Bible where the Son of God pulls back the veil and lets us peer way down into the core of who he is, we are not told that he is 'austere and demanding in heart.' We are not told that he is 'exalted and dignified in heart.' We are not even told that he is 'joyful and generous in heart.' Letting Jesus set the terms, his surprising claim is that he is 'gentle and lowly in heart.'"

Gentle. Not harsh or reactive.
Lowly. Not inaccessible or aloof.

This is how Christ describes his inner life—the posture he takes toward sinners and sufferers, toward the weary and burdened. He does not recoil. He doesn't stand over us with folded arms. His heart moves toward us. His words make space for us. His tone invites rest, not resistance.

And if this is the way Jesus speaks to us, it shapes how we are to speak to others.

To grow in gentleness is not to become timid. It is to become like Jesus.

Gentleness Is Not Softness

Of course, not everyone sees gentleness as strength.

In a world that prizes dominance and visibility, gentleness is often dismissed as weakness. It can feel soft, passive, and even naïve. We live in a culture where volume equals power, where assertiveness is rewarded, and where the loudest voice often gets the final say. So, when someone leads with tenderness instead of force, they're often seen as less capable—or worse, easily ignored.

But that's not the biblical view; that's the world's view.

Gentleness is not the absence of power. It is *power restrained in love.* It is courage with a soft edge and strength with an open hand. It takes far more internal strength to remain gentle under pressure than it does to explode in anger or shut down in fear. Anyone can react. But gentleness *chooses* a different way.

It's the parent who disciplines without shaming. The leader who listens before speaking. The person who has every right to strike back but instead leaves room for peace.

To live with gentleness is not to shrink back. Gentleness shows up with the quiet confidence of someone who knows they are secure in Christ. Gentleness is the fruit of a will that has been surrendered to God.

And that kind of courage is anything but weak.

Gentleness is holding back harshness even when it's deserved. Lowering your voice when everything in you wants to raise it.

Seeing the vulnerability in others and choosing to protect rather than expose.

When Paul lists the fruit of the Spirit in Galatians 5, gentleness is near the end of the list. But it is not an afterthought. It is a culmination—a fruit that blossoms when our lives are rooted in the Spirit of Christ. And Christ himself shows us what that fruit looks like, not just in action but in tone, in posture, and in heart.

Beyond Guilt

The gentleness of Jesus takes shape in real moments, with real people, often in the wake of real failure.

Perhaps nowhere is this more vividly seen than in John 21.

Peter had failed. Not just in a private moment of doubt or distraction, but in the very hour Jesus needed him most. "I don't know the man," he had said (not once, but three times), warming his hands over a charcoal fire while his Lord stood trial only yards away. He had promised undying loyalty. He had drawn a sword in the garden. But when the pressure came, he crumbled.

And then Jesus rose from the dead.

It's hard to imagine what Peter must have felt in the days that followed. Joy, yes, but likely also shame. He had seen the empty tomb. He had even seen the risen Christ. But nothing had been said. There was no conversation, no reckoning, no restoration. Just silence.

Until a morning on the shore.

The disciples had returned to Galilee and gone fishing—perhaps unsure of what else to do. After a long, empty night on the water, a man called out to them from the shore, telling them to cast the net on the other side. They did—and the nets filled with fish. John was the first to recognize what was happening. "It is the Lord," he said. Peter jumped into the water.

When they reached the shore, they saw a charcoal fire burning—just like the one Peter had stood beside on the night of his denial. The detail is no accident. Jesus had recreated the scene, but not to trap Peter in guilt. He had made breakfast.

He had created space for the Spirit to work in Peter.

After they had eaten, Jesus turned to Peter. Not with a lecture and not with a list of what he had done wrong. Instead, he asked a question: "Simon son of John, do you love me?"

Three times he asked. One for each denial.

But notice the tone. Jesus did not say, "Do you regret what you've done?" He didn't demand, "Will you promise to do better?" He asked about love. He restored Peter with gentleness, not guilt. He gave him a chance to speak again—not words of betrayal, but words of devotion.

Each time Peter responded, Jesus gave him a task: "Feed my sheep." He didn't just forgive Peter. He entrusted him with the care of others. He didn't merely let Peter back in. He commissioned him forward.

This is what gentleness does.

It doesn't ignore failure, but it doesn't weaponize it either.
It doesn't erase pain; instead, it creates a safe space for healing.
It doesn't shrink from the truth, but it delivers that truth with grace.

In Jesus' hands, gentleness is strong enough to confront and soft enough to restore. And in Peter's story, we see both. We see a Savior who doesn't just erase the past but rewrites it. Jesus meets his friend at the place of deepest shame and gently speaks life over him again.

Evidence That Demands a Verdict

After breakfast by the sea, after the fire and the forgiveness, Jesus sent Peter back into the world with a calling shaped by gentleness. "Feed my sheep," he said. Not "straighten them out." Not "make them behave." Feed them. Care for them. Shepherd them with the same heart that had just restored his own.

The apostle Paul would later write to the church in Philippi, urging them with a strikingly simple command: "Let your gentleness be evident to all" (Philippians 4:5).

Let it be obvious. Let it be known. Let it leave a trail behind you.

Eugene Peterson tells a story from when his kids were young, during a summer vacation in a national park. They were hiking through an alpine meadow—a place bursting with wildflowers of every kind. Meadows like that are fragile, sacred spaces, and it's illegal to pick the flowers. But a six-year-old girl, walking a few steps ahead of her family, didn't know that. With innocent delight, she was gathering a bouquet for her mother, plucking flower after flower in wide-eyed joy.

Peterson, seeing this, responded with his "big preacher voice," as he later described it. He sternly rebuked the child, warning her that what she was doing was against the rules. The little girl froze, dropped the flowers, burst into tears, and ran to her parents.

His own family, appalled, turned on him. "You can't talk to a child like that," they said.

In his book *Subversive Spirituality*, Peterson reflects on the moment—not only agreeing with them but going further: "You cannot yell people into holiness. You cannot terrify people into the sacred. My yelling was a far worse violation of the holy place than her picking a few flowers. I do that a lot—bluster and yell on behalf of God's holy presence instead of taking off my shoes myself, kneeling on holy ground, and inviting whoever happens to be around to join with me."

It wasn't about the rule. It was about the spirit in which it was enforced. In that moment, a preacher's indignation rang louder than a little girl's beauty-filled impulse.

And it raises the question: Is your gentleness evident to everyone around you?

If someone followed you for a day—through your errands, into your workplace, around your dinner table—would "gentle" be one of the first words they'd use to describe you?

Too often in the church, we convince ourselves that being right justifies everything. We speak the truth but without love. We act in the name of holiness but without humility. We think we're doing the Lord's work, but we're using the devil's tone.

But that's not the way of Jesus. Contrary to what is often prized in our political arena today from both sides of the political spectrum, anger is not a fruit of the Spirit. Neither is outrage.
Righteousness never requires cruelty. And truth never needs to shout.

If we want to join Jesus in the work of feeding his sheep, we must learn to lay down our clenched fists and raise open hands. Peace does not come through raised volume. It begins with gentleness—spirit-breathed, Spirit-shaped gentleness—with the people right in front of us.

Addicted

Gentleness lives in the way we speak, inhabiting the words we choose, the tone we carry, and the restraint we show when provoked. But in an age of endless commentary and instant reaction, it often feels like gentleness doesn't stand a chance.

Rabbi Joseph Telushkin, in his book *Words That Hurt, Words That Heal*, addresses this struggle head-on. As he traveled to speak about the power of words, he would often open his seminars with a challenge: "Raise your hand if you believe you can go twenty-four hours without saying an unkind word about another person."

Some would raise their hands, cautiously confident. Others would laugh nervously and shake their heads. No way, they'd say. Not a chance.

Telushkin called it his "twenty-four-hour challenge." Then he would deliver the insight that stayed with people long after the seminar ended: "Those who can't answer 'yes' must recognize that you have a serious problem. If you cannot go twenty-four hours without drinking alcohol, you are addicted to alcohol. If you cannot go twenty-four hours without smoking, you are addicted to nicotine. And if you cannot go twenty-four hours without speaking unkind words, then you have lost control over your tongue."

This is where many of us live. We raise our hands, shrug our shoulders, and say, "It's not possible. It's not realistic." And we surrender to a world of sarcasm, cynicism, and outrage as if it were inevitable.

But it isn't.

Telushkin tells another story, this one from Eastern Europe. A man in a small village had spoken falsely about a local rabbi. The words were unkind, unnecessary, and untrue. Eventually, the man's conscience caught up with him. He went to the rabbi and asked for forgiveness, offering to do whatever it would take to make things right.

The rabbi gave him a task.

"Go home," he said, "and bring me the pillow from your bed. Then go outside into the street, rip it open, and return."

The man did as he was told. He opened the pillow, and the wind carried its feathers in every direction—floating down alleys, into trees, across rooftops.

He returned to the rabbi and said, "I did what you asked. Am I forgiven now?"

"Not yet," the rabbi said. "Now go gather every feather and place them all back into the pillow."

The man looked at him, stricken. "But that's impossible."

The rabbi nodded. "So it is with your words."

When we speak in haste or harm, we scatter what cannot be easily recovered. Even when forgiven, the damage remains. The wounds echo.

But by grace we follow a different rabbi.

There is One we have wronged—not with gossip alone, but with pride and carelessness, with words hurled in frustration and silence held in fear. We come to him with empty hands, asking, "Is there anything I can do?"

And this rabbi does not send us away with a task we cannot complete.

He says instead, "Come to me. I will gather every feather. I will carry every careless word. I will forgive, and I will restore."

Jesus does not shame us into silence. He invites us into a better way.

We live in an age where words fly faster than ever before—online, in texts, in whispered conversations and public platforms. Whether you speak seven thousand words a day or thirty thousand, each one matters. And each one is a chance to reflect the Spirit of the One who is gentle and lowly in heart.

Our words will hurt, but God's words through you can heal.

And so the question remains: *What will you say next?*

An Invitation for Reflection & Growth

KEY VERSE

A gentle answer turns away wrath,
but a harsh word stirs up anger.
—Proverbs 15:1

BIG IDEA

Gentleness is not weakness—it's strength under control. It carries burdens, disarms pride, calms conflict, and restores the broken. In a world of sharp edges and quick tempers, gentleness is a powerful witness to the heart of Christ, who speaks tenderly and stoops low to lift others up.

READING & REFLECTION

Gentleness That Carries

Read Matthew 11:28–30 and Proverbs 15:1

- What does it mean that Jesus is "gentle and humble in heart"?
- How does gentleness lighten the load both for you and others?

Reflection & Practice

- Where do you need to receive his rest—or offer it to someone else?
- Think of one person whose burdens you can help carry this week. Then, reach out to them in gentleness.

Gentleness That Defuses

Read Proverbs 15:1 and 2 Kings 5:1–14

- How do Naaman's servants respond to his anger and pride?
- What makes their gentle words so powerful?

Reflection & Practice

- Where might gentleness calm a conflict in your life?
- Pray for wisdom to speak softly where you've been tempted to escalate. Choose calm over control.

Gentleness That Witnesses

Read Philippians 4:4–7

- How does Paul connect gentleness with joy, prayer, and peace?
- What does public gentleness look like in everyday life?

Reflection & Practice

- Where can your gentleness be a witness to God's nearness?
- Ask yourself: *What does gentleness look like in me today?* Let it shape how you speak, post, and respond.

Gentleness That Restores

Read Galatians 6:1–5

- What posture does Paul call for when restoring someone caught in sin?
- Why is gentleness essential in both correction and care?

Reflection & Practice

- Where have you experienced restoration through gentleness? Was it more long-lasting?

- Think of someone who needs grace more than judgment. Pray for them—and be ready to help be part of the story that makes that a reality.

CULTIVATION PRACTICE: SOFTEN THE TONE

Choose one recurring conversation—at home, at work, or even online—that tends to be routine, challenging, or emotionally charged. This week, focus not just on *what* you say, but *how* you say it. Let your tone carry the fruit of the Spirit, especially gentleness. Reflect with these guiding questions:

- Am I speaking to win or to restore?
- Am I offering truth in love or just unloading truth?
- Does my tone invite trust, or does it shut it down?

Let this simple, ordinary exchange become sacred ground. And remember the words of Philippians 4:5—"Let your gentleness be evident to all."

A PRAYER TO CULTIVATE GENTLENESS

Jesus, you are gentle and lowly in heart—
not because you are weak,
but because you are love.

You speak with truth,
but never with cruelty.
You confront,
but never condemn.

You restore what shame would destroy.

So shape my heart to be like yours.

Teach me to lower my voice
when I want to raise it.
To pause before I speak,
to listen longer than I want to,
to see the person behind the mistake,
the wound behind the word.

I've scattered too many feathers—
with sarcasm, with silence,
with words meant more to win than to heal.
I've spoken when I should have waited,
and stayed quiet when love should have spoken.

Forgive me.
And begin again in me.

Give me the strength to be tender.
The courage to be kind.
The wisdom to use my words not as weapons,
but as invitations.

Let my tone reflect your mercy.
Let my posture echo your compassion.
Let my speech bear the weight of your grace.

In every conversation,
with every word,
make me more like you.

Amen.

INTERLUDE

TAKE STOCK

When Paul lists the fruit of the Spirit in Galatians 5, he doesn't do so at random. Nor does he give us a buffet of options to pick and choose what we like. These nine virtues—love, joy, peace, patience, kindness, goodness, faithfulness, gentleness, and self-control—are not merely admirable traits or aspirational goals. They are visible evidence of the life of God growing in us.

Not Just a List

Some people try to read too much into the order. They might say, "Love comes first because it's the greatest," or, "Self-control comes last because it's the hardest." Others might look for a tidy theological logic: The first three are directed toward God, the second three toward others, the last three toward ourselves.

There's some truth in those patterns. But if we press them too far, we risk missing the forest for the trees. Paul didn't write a systematic theology here—he wrote to a church struggling to live in the freedom of the Spirit instead of the two extremes of falling back into law or sliding into license.

That said, we also shouldn't under-interpret the order. Paul was intentional. This is fruit, not an individual checklist. There is an organic flow, a cultivation of character that builds over time. Love roots us. Joy springs up. Peace settles in. Patience slows us down. Kindness leans outward. Goodness holds firm. Faithfulness stays. Gentleness softens. Self-control steadies. Each one prepares the soil for the next.

All or None

It's also important to note that Paul says, "The fruit of the Spirit *is* . . ." Not *are*. It's singular. That's not bad grammar; it's good theology. The Spirit doesn't produce nine different fruits depending on your personality type or your ministry setting. This isn't a spiritual Myers-Briggs.

The fruit is one. It's unified. Interconnected. Like the facets of a diamond or the parts of a body. You can't fully grow in one without being shaped in the others.

You can't have love without patience. You can't have gentleness without self-control. You can't truly express kindness without joy. If you try to isolate them, they begin to wither.

What the Spirit cultivates in us is not perfection in categories, but a wholeness of character. A life formed in Christ. And like fruit, it takes time. Growth is gradual. But it is also inevitable when rooted in the Spirit.

An Invitation, Not a Demand

The fruit of the Spirit is not a list of things we must produce to prove ourselves. It's the evidence of who we're becoming as we walk in step with the Spirit. It is both a gift and a call.

So, let's take a moment.

Where do you see this fruit growing in your life? Maybe not perfectly. Maybe not every day. But where has the Spirit made you more loving? Where has joy returned? Where have you shown surprising patience or spoken with new gentleness?

Celebrate that. It's evidence of God's living presence in you. Thank him for it.

And then, with honesty and hope, ask: *Where is the fruit missing or immature? Is there a part of my character still struggling to bloom?*

Don't respond with shame. Respond with intention.

Offer that part of your heart to the Spirit's care. Ask for help and pay attention. Water it with prayer. Tend it with truth. Practice it with effort. This is how fruit grows—in the soil of grace and in the rhythm of daily surrender.

Because the Spirit is not finished with you yet. And the One who began a good work in you will be faithful to complete it.

CHAPTER 9

SELF-CONTROL

The One Who Trains You

Our dog, Shasta, was energy personified.

He was high-octane from the moment we got him—eager, adventuresome, and strong-willed. Taking him on a walk wasn't peaceful or leisurely; it was a tug-of-war. He pulled on the leash with all the force his muscular frame could muster. A quick neighborhood stroll turned into a power struggle, with me bracing against the tension and Shasta lunging forward, convinced there was something better just around the corner.

No matter what we tried, whether it was changing leashes, using treats, or stopping to reset, every walk was a battle of wills. He was smart. He could do the basics: sit, down, stay (for about two seconds). But out in the real world, with distractions and squirrels and smells, those tricks vanished. I wasn't walking the dog. The dog was walking me.

Then one day, we were at the mall, and I saw a man at a kiosk advertising dog-training services. He had a bulldog calmly sitting next to him, wearing a pair of sunglasses like he belonged on a beach in Malibu. The sign read, "Loose-leash training in 15 minutes—Money-back guarantee."

I laughed out loud.

Fifteen minutes? No way. He had clearly never met our dog.

I told him about Shasta—how I could take him on a full-speed bike ride, and he'd get home barely winded, looking at me like, *Is that all you've got?* The trainer smiled and said, "Let me come to your house."

So he did.

When he arrived, he asked me to show him what Shasta could do. I pulled out a few treats, ran through the usual routine . . . sit, down, shake. Shasta performed them, more or less. The trainer nodded. Then he pulled out a special training leash, adjusted it with practiced hands, and within five minutes Shasta was calmly walking at his side, focused and responsive.

I stood there in shock.

We sat down at the dining table afterward, and the trainer told me something I haven't forgotten: "Your dog," he said, "knows some tricks. But he's not trained. You're not in control. He is."

That sentence hit me harder than expected. Because it wasn't just about the dog anymore.

It was about me. And it's about many of us.

In the Christian life, it's possible to know all the right moves. We can go through the motions like praying before meals, reciting familiar verses, and showing up on Sunday mornings. We know the tricks. But when the pressure comes, when temptation hits or emotions rise, we're off the leash. We lunge forward, pulled by impulse, desire, anger, fear.

Self-control isn't about knowing spiritual tricks. It's about being trained, shaped, submitted, and disciplined by the Spirit of God. And until that happens, we may look obedient in moments, but we're still in charge. We're still walking ourselves.

But what if the Spirit's work in us is not just about belief, but about *training*? What if bearing fruit means surrendering control and letting God take the lead?

Here's what we tend to forget: Self-control isn't generated from us but formed by the Spirit within us. It's something God cultivates in us until our lives begin to match the gentle rhythm of his steps.

Let the Games Begin

The apostle Paul understood the value of training. And he knew how to speak the language of a culture that prized performance, discipline, and public glory.

To understand the weight of his words in 1 Corinthians 9, it helps to remember where he was writing. Corinth was home to one of the most prominent athletic festivals in the ancient world—the Isthmian Games, second only to the Olympics in prestige. Held every two years just outside the city, these games featured footraces, wrestling, chariot races, boxing, and more. Athletes came from all over the Roman Empire to compete.

But they didn't just show up and hope for the best.

Participation in the games required *ten months of documented training.* Athletes lived under strict discipline, often away from home, with their diet, sleep, and routines monitored. They trained not just to perform, but to *win*. And all for the sake of a crown—literally, a wreath made of pine or celery—that would wither within days.

This is the context behind Paul's words: "Do you not know that in a race all the runners run, but only one gets the prize? Run in such a way as to get the prize. Everyone who competes in the games goes into strict training. They do it to get a crown that will not last, but we do it to get a crown that will last forever. Therefore I do not run like someone running aimlessly; I do not fight like a boxer beating the air. No, I strike a blow to my body and make it my slave so that after I have preached to others, I myself will not be disqualified for the prize" (1 Corinthians 9:24–27).

This isn't Paul being legalistic or joyless. He's not obsessed with self-denial. He's reminding the Corinthian church—and us—that following Jesus is not a passive, casual pursuit. It takes focus and effort, its own kind of spiritual conditioning.

Paul knew the human heart. He understood how quickly good intentions can be undone by undisciplined desires. He knew that the ability to say *no* to impulse or *yes* to obedience doesn't come from a flash of inspiration. It comes from training.

It comes from *cultivation*.

Just like fruit doesn't grow overnight, neither does character. It must be tended, nurtured, and shaped over time. The kind of self-control Paul describes is not stiff willpower or white-knuckled restraint. It is the mature fruit that grows when the Spirit has been shaping every part of us.

Self-control is not a standalone virtue. It's the overflow of a life already being formed by love and joy, by peace and patience, by kindness, goodness, faithfulness, and gentleness. Each one of these prepares the ground for the kind of self-restraint that is not reactive, but responsive. Not forced, but free.

Love tells us what to hold on to.
Joy tells us what to pursue.
Peace keeps us grounded when everything else pulls.
Patience teaches us to wait when we'd rather rush.
Kindness and goodness shape how we act when no one's watching.
Faithfulness keeps us consistent.
Gentleness softens our strength.

And self-control? It holds all of that together. It is the fruit that makes all the other fruit visible in real life—especially when tested.

Paul isn't chasing perfection. He's chasing the prize—life with God, fully surrendered. And he wants his daily choices, his habits, his words, and his body to match that pursuit.

So do we.

Training in the Wilderness

We are not alone in this.

Even Jesus, the One who was perfectly obedient, didn't bypass the need for training. His life was not a constant stream of miracles and easy answers. It was a life formed through hidden preparation, quiet obedience, and sustained resistance.

The cross wasn't automatic. Gethsemane wasn't effortless. The self-control Jesus displayed in his final hours didn't just appear in that moment. It was the fruit of a life that had already been tested—and had held.

Right after his baptism, before he preached a single sermon or healed a single person, Jesus was led by the Spirit into the wilderness. For forty days, he fasted. He was alone. Hungry. Weak. Vulnerable. And that's where the enemy came not with brute force, but with temptation. With subtle lies. With shortcuts to power.

"Turn these stones into bread."
"Throw yourself down and prove who you are."
"Bow down, and I'll give you all the kingdoms of the world."

Each of these offers touched something real: physical hunger, public recognition, worldly control. But Jesus resisted. Not by gritting his teeth, but by returning to what was true. Each time, he answered with Scripture. He stood firm, not because it was easy, but because he was ready.

He had trained for this.

A friend of mine likes to say that the typical American church is "over-programmed and under-discipled." We tend to treat spiritual formation like it's automatic—like it happens through exposure, not intentionality. We think the problem is that we're not trying hard enough. But the real problem is that we don't think of ourselves as *students*—as disciples who are being trained.

The Greek word for disciple, *mathetes*, doesn't mean "fan" or "attendee." It means "learner," "apprentice," or "one who is shaped."

Jesus didn't come simply to forgive our sins. He came to form our lives. He came to teach us how to live in the rhythms of grace and truth. And just like the wilderness wasn't optional for Jesus, formation isn't optional for us. If we want to bear the fruit of self-control, we have to train.

Not in our own strength. Not to earn anything. But because we're learning to walk in step with the Spirit.

It takes time. It takes intention. But it leads to a life where, slowly and surely, we are no longer driven by impulse but led by love.

The Aligned Life of Jesus

One of the reasons we are drawn to Jesus is that his life is so completely aligned. His words and actions match. His values and choices are integrated. His will is not divided. He doesn't say one thing and do another. He doesn't make excuses or live with hidden duplicity. In him, there is a rare wholeness—a clarity of life—that we instinctively recognize as good.

This is not only moral perfection. It is *self-control* at its deepest expression.

Because Jesus does not react out of impulse. He doesn't respond from ego. Under pressure or scrutiny, he acts with restraint, mercy, and authority. Whether he is being tested in the wilderness, surrounded by angry crowds, betrayed by a friend, or mocked on the cross, he stays rooted in who he is. He knows what he's doing. He is fully submitted to the Father's will.

And it's that alignment—between identity and action, between conviction and behavior—that reveals his character.

That same alignment is what the Spirit cultivates in us.

We were not created to live fragmented lives where people encounter one version of ourselves at work, another at home, and a third in private. We were made to be whole. And self-control is what restores that wholeness. It is the Spirit's way of bringing our thoughts, desires, words, and habits into alignment with the life of Christ.

The Habit Gap

All of this, the story of Shasta, Paul's training metaphor, the wilderness testing of Jesus, points us to one overlooked but deeply important truth:

Much of your life is not the result of conscious decision.

According to behavioral researchers, including Charles Duhigg in his best-selling book *The Power of Habit*, about 40 percent of what you do in a given day is not the result of deliberate choice but of unconscious routine. Nearly half of your waking hours are spent on autopilot.

And that's where many of us get stuck. We want to change. We want to grow. But we underestimate how deeply formed we already are—by our environment, our habits, our default settings. We try to will ourselves into transformation while ignoring the structures that shape us every day.

This is the neglected frontier of discipleship: *habit*.

We've taught people to believe in Jesus. We've even taught them to try to behave a certain way. But we haven't trained them to build a life that *automatically aligns with Jesus*—one that, over time, defaults toward love, patience, restraint, courage.

Duhigg writes that habits follow a predictable loop: *cue* → *routine* → *reward*. Once that loop is established, it becomes almost automatic. The trick isn't just to try harder but to *interrupt the loop* and replace the old routine with a new one—one that leads to life, not emptiness.

The good news is that this is exactly how the Spirit works.

Spiritual formation is not magic. It is not instant, but it is transformational. The Spirit partners with us in forming new rhythms, new instincts, new defaults. And over time, what once required enormous effort becomes second nature.

Self-control begins when we stop relying on inspiration and start cooperating with cultivation. It's not about perfection. It's about being *retrained* bit by bit, day by day, in the Spirit's gym.

This is why ancient Christians built daily rhythms of prayer and fasting. It's why Jesus withdrew regularly to quiet places. It's why Paul spoke of presenting his body—not just his thoughts—as a living sacrifice.

Because formation happens in the ordinary.
In your calendar. In your conversations. In your habits.

And if 40 percent of your life is shaped by unconscious patterns, then discipleship must reach into those places. It must press past belief into *behavioral muscle memory*. Because when the pressure comes (and it always does), we don't rise to the level of our intentions. We fall to the level of our training.

Training for Freedom: Habits That Shape the Soul

If self-control is the Spirit's fruit and training is the pathway, then it makes sense to begin by examining the daily patterns that shape us. Not to obsess over performance but to become more aware, more intentional, and more available to the Spirit's forming work.

Here are a few simple, practical ways to begin cooperating with the Spirit in cultivating self-control:

1. Name the Pattern That Has You

Before you can train a new habit, you must recognize the old one. Where are you most likely to lose control of your words, your emotions, your appetites, your time? Is it a late-night scroll that always ends in shame? Is it a conversation that always turns sarcastic? Is it a calendar that never makes space for rest?

Pay attention to the cue, the routine, and the reward. Then ask the Spirit to help you identify where a holy interruption might begin.

2. Start Smaller Than You Think

One of the biggest mistakes people make in forming new habits is trying to do too much, too fast. Spiritual disciplines, like any form of training, require humility and sustainability. Don't aim for a dramatic overhaul. Begin with one act of surrender: Five minutes of prayer before reaching for your phone. A Scripture card taped to your mirror. A breath prayer when you feel the first wave of frustration rise.

Remember: We're not trying to impress God. We're letting him reshape us.

3. Choose Structure That Sets You Free

Our culture associates freedom with the absence of constraints. But biblical freedom is the ability to choose what is good, even when it's hard. That kind of freedom grows in the soil of discipline.

This is why Christians across centuries have practiced things like *Sabbath*, *fasting*, and *fixed-hour prayer.* These aren't legalistic rules. They're loving boundaries that retrain your soul. Try setting up daily anchors—simple, repeating practices that re-center your attention on God throughout the day.

4. Use Your Body to Train Your Heart

Paul said, "I discipline my body and keep it under control" (1 Corinthians 9:27 ESV). He knew that spiritual maturity wasn't just an internal mindset—it showed up in the body. In habits. In posture. In presence.

Try praying with your body: Kneel to confess. Open your hands to receive. Go for a walk without your phone. Fast from something that usually masters you, such as food, social media, or caffeine. And allow your body to remember that it is not in charge.

5. Invite Community into Your Formation

Training is never meant to be solitary. Even Jesus had companions on the way. We need people who will not only hold us accountable, but hold us up.

Find someone to walk with you in your training, whether that's a friend, a mentor, or a small group. Share the habits you're hoping to build or break. Celebrate progress, not perfection. Encourage one another daily, as Hebrews says, "so that none of you may be hardened by sin's deceitfulness" (3:13).

Self-control is not just about holding back. It's about being held together—by the Spirit who trains you, the Savior who models the way, and the community that helps you stay the course.

How We Change

Imagine you have a friend—someone respected at work, active at church, admired by others. But at home, something's off. He's impatient. Easily irritated. His words land too hard. He's not abusive, but his tone wears down the people he loves most.

One night, his teenage daughter leaves a note on his pillow: "I love you. But I don't know how to talk to you anymore."

It wrecks him.

The next day, he starts to change. Not with a big speech. Not with a dramatic vow. He starts by naming the pattern of anger, control, defensiveness, and invites the Spirit to interrupt it.

He starts small: A sticky note on the mirror. A breath prayer before speaking. Five minutes of Scripture before checking his phone. He chooses structure: a weekly fast—not from food, but from criticism. He uses his body to train his heart—kneeling to pray, walking in silence. And he invites community in. He asks his wife and daughter to tell him when he slips, and he listens—without getting defensive.

Over time, the changes stick. He isn't just controlling his reactions. He's becoming someone different. Someone safe.

Years later, his daughter writes a new note: "Thank you for becoming someone I can talk to."

That's the quiet power and impact of Spirit-shaped self-control.

Trained for the Moment

Several years ago, some friends from out of town came to visit, and we took them to Disneyland. All of our kiddos were thrilled to be selected for the Jedi Training Academy.

Here's how it works: First, you're chosen. Then they hand you a brown robe and a plastic lightsaber. Next, you're brought onstage and taught how to use it. At first, it seems like nothing more than a fun photo op. But just as the kids start to settle into the routine, the Stormtroopers arrive. And then Darth Vader himself appears. One by one, each new "Jedi" gets a turn to fight him.

But on the day we were there, the weather changed. It didn't pour, not even a light rain. Just a fine mist. A spritzing, really.

Disney quickly canceled the performance.

Instead of facing Darth Vader, the kids were ushered straight to the graduation ceremony to receive their Jedi certificate. The whole thing was over before it had even started.

And the kids were disappointed.

They knew the robes and lightsabers weren't the point. They weren't there to go through the motions. They came to be trained. To stand up to darkness. To be part of something bigger than themselves.

And I couldn't help but wonder: *How many people's experience of Christianity is like that Jedi Training Academy?*

We put on the robe. We swing the sword a few times. We attend the ceremony. But when things get hard—when pressure comes or the weather turns—we settle for a baptism certificate instead of grace-filled transformation.

We were never meant to just dress the part.
We were never meant to treat discipleship like a spiritual beach day.
We were meant to be trained for something real. Something that matters.

Because the battle is real. And there is nothing like being ready for it.

The Fruit of Training

During the early days of the 2020 COVID-19 pandemic, when hospitals were overwhelmed and respirators were in short supply, a story emerged from a small village in Northern Italy.

Casnigo is a quiet, charming town in the foothills of the Italian Alps. It's the kind of place where everyone knows everyone. One of the most beloved figures in the town was a seventy-two-year-old priest named Father Giuseppe Berardelli. He was known for his kindness, his joy, and the way he rode his little red scooter through the streets.

When COVID struck Italy, it hit hard. Father Berardelli fell seriously ill and was taken to the hospital. A respirator had been secured for him by friends and parishioners who wanted to ensure he had the best chance of surviving. But when he learned that a younger patient and someone he didn't even know was also in need, he quietly gave the respirator away.

He died days later.

How does someone become like that?

How does a person have the presence of mind—and the selflessness of heart—to make that kind of decision?

It doesn't happen automatically. And it doesn't happen overnight.

It happens when a life has been shaped day by day, prayer by prayer, habit by habit, by the love of Christ. It happens when self-control is not about trying harder, but about surrendering deeper. It happens when, like Paul, like Jesus, like so many who have gone before us, we stop living for temporary crowns and start living for something eternal.

Father Berardelli didn't make a heroic decision in a single moment. He had been training for it his whole life.

As James Clear popularized in his book *Atomic Habits*, we don't rise to the level of our expectations, we fall to the level of our training.

And so, we train.

Not because we're earning anything.
Not because we're strong.
But because the Spirit is cultivating a life within us that is ready—ready to stand, to speak, to love, to give.

Self-control isn't about control for its own sake.
It's about *freedom*.
The freedom to respond instead of react.

The freedom to give rather than grasp.
The freedom to choose what is right even when it costs you everything.

And that kind of freedom?
It's worth the investment.

An Invitation for Reflection & Growth

KEY VERSE

Like a city whose walls are broken through
is a person who lacks self-control.
—Proverbs 25:28

BIG IDEA

Self-control is not about suppressing your desires—it's about being trained by the Spirit to direct them. It's the discipline to resist what harms us, the wisdom to pause before reacting, and the courage to keep running when others quit. In Christ, we are being shaped to live with purpose, freedom, and strength.

READING & REFLECTION

Self-Control That Guards

Read Proverbs 25:28 and Luke 22:47–53

- How does Peter act impulsively? How does Jesus respond?

- What does this contrast highlight and teach you about true strength?

Reflection & Practice

- Where do you need God's help to guard what matters most?
- Ask yourself: *Where am I reacting instead of responding?* Invite Jesus to steady your spirit today.

Self-Control That Resists

Read Genesis 39:1–12

- How does Joseph respond to temptation? What empowers his choice?
- What's the cost of resisting? What's the reward?

Reflection & Practice

- Where are you being tempted to trade long-term calling for short-term comfort?
- Name one place where you need the strength to say no. Ask the Spirit to train your will for what's better.

Self-Control That Speaks Wisely

Read James 3:1–12

- What does James say about the power—and danger—of the tongue?
- How do words reveal what's going on inside us?

Reflection & Practice

- Where do you need to pause and let wisdom lead your speech?
- Practice silence for five minutes today. Let God speak to your heart before you speak to others.

Self-Control That Wins

Read 1 Corinthians 9:24–27

- How does Paul describe the Christian life as disciplined training?
- What helps you stay focused when you want to give up?

Reflection & Practice

- Where is God inviting you to keep showing up?
- Write down one habit you want to cultivate and one distraction you need to resist. Ask God to help you run with purpose.

CULTIVATION PRACTICE: TRAIN THE HEART

Draw a simple target with three rings, moving from the outside inward:

- **Outer Ring:** Habits that need pruning and patterns that may be bearing fruit, but not the kind that lasts.
- **Middle Ring:** Distractions that need boundaries or places where your time, attention, or energy are being slowly drained.
- **Center Ring:** Desires that need realignment, or longings that may be good but need to be reoriented toward God's heart and purposes.

Spend time in prayer this week, sitting with what you've named. Don't rush to fix or manage. Instead, invite the Holy Spirit to do the deeper work by not just reshaping your behavior, but retraining your desires and attention. Spiritual formation isn't just about what you *stop doing*. It's about becoming the kind of person whose heart beats in rhythm with God's.

A PRAYER TO CULTIVATE SELF-CONTROL

Spirit of the Living God,
I confess—
I am too easily pulled.
By impulse, by fear, by distraction, by pride.
I know the right thing,
but too often, I reach for the easy one.

Train me.

Not just to perform spiritual tricks,
but to walk in step with you when no one is watching.
Shape me slowly, steadily—like roots deepening underground.
Build strength in the quiet places,
discipline in the daily ones.

Interrupt my reflexes.
Rewire my habits.
Form in me a heart that listens before reacting,
chooses what is good when comfort would be easier,
and surrenders to your pace when mine would rush ahead.

I don't want to just look the part.
I want to be ready.

When the pressure comes—
when temptation whispers, when anger sparks,
when fatigue dulls my judgment or fear clouds my mind—
let your Spirit speak louder.

Let me remember:
You are not asking for perfection.
You are inviting me to rely on your grace
for every moment.

Make me faithful in the small things
so I might stand in the moment that matters most.

Amen.

CONCLUSION

THE GRAND PRIZE

Years ago, our family lived in the New York City area and supported a remarkable organization committed to planting churches and spreading the gospel throughout the city. One statistic stunned me: At that time, two-thirds of all pastors in the New York metro area had no formal theological education. These were faithful, passionate men and women, many of whom had never had the chance to be taught, mentored, or formed in ministry.

So we found ourselves at a gala fundraiser in one of Manhattan's grand ballrooms to help pastors with more training. It sparkled with chandeliers and ambition. To raise support, they raffled off extravagant experiences: romantic dinners at the Water Club with sweeping city views, breakfast in the Rainbow Room atop Rockefeller Center, a weekend getaway to Nantucket, a long weekend in Bermuda, a weeklong Caribbean vacation in the dead of winter.

I had bought only one ticket. Just one. I missed out on all of the above.

As they read off the grand prize winner's ticket number, it exactly matched the number on my single raffle ticket. I couldn't believe it. Fist in the air, spotlight on me, applause all around. I strode toward the stage, ready for ocean breezes and island sun.

They handed me a leather-bound study Bible.

I already had a dozen.

I smiled—sort of. They handed me a microphone, expecting something meaningful. But I had nothing. Just a weak "Thank you" as I carried the Bible back to my seat like a consolation prize.

And that's when I heard it, quiet but unmistakable.

Rich, do you believe this is the grand prize?

The Spirit wasn't mocking me. He was inviting me. Inviting me to reconsider what I prize and truly value. In that moment, the honest answer was no. I was valuing the wrong thing.

I wanted the escape, not the Word.

And yet that gentle rebuke turned out to be a window into something deeper:
Our greatest challenge in spiritual formation may not be a lack of faith.
It may be a lack of imagination.

Dallas Willard once said, "Our problem with Scripture today is our imagination, not a lack of understanding." That rings true. In a world formed by distraction, cynicism, and instant gratification, we have forgotten how to see. We've lost the ability to envision what life could be like—should be like—when shaped by the Spirit.

Warehouse Living

Karl Barth once gave his students a parable. Imagine a group of people who have lived their entire lives inside a massive warehouse. They're born there. Raised there. Everything they need is inside. Food, light, shelter. And while the building has windows, they're thick with dust—never cleaned, never used.

One day, a child pulls a stool to the window and scrapes away the grime. What he sees astonishes him: people walking on streets, a world beyond the warehouse. He calls to his friends, and they crowd around the window, wide-eyed. But then they notice the people outside are looking *up*. They're pointing and talking excitedly.

The warehouse children look up too—but all they see is their own ceiling. Eventually, they get bored. They dismiss the people outside as fools pointing at nothing.

But of course, they weren't pointing at nothing.
They were pointing at the skies.

Barth's point is that studying Scripture, entering into the story of God, is like stepping outside the warehouse. It opens up new dimensions, new beauty, new horizons. The life we've settled for is not enough—not big enough, not rich enough—for the joy and glory God wants to give us.

That's the invitation.

To cultivate a life that stretches beyond the warehouse.

To imagine a world shaped not by scarcity, fear, and striving—but by the fruit of the Spirit.

Love.
Joy.
Peace.
Patience.
Kindness.
Goodness.
Faithfulness.
Gentleness.
Self-control.

This is not a list of goals to achieve. It is the fruit of a life rooted in God's presence and formed by his grace.

We've looked at love that abides. Joy that breaks into silence. Peace that stills our storms. Patience that trusts in the slow work of God. Kindness that responds to pain. Goodness that shines even in tragedy. Faithfulness that keeps its promises. Gentleness that honors others. And self-control that surrenders to the Spirit.

Mike's Story

Author Gary Thomas recounts the story of an upperclassman he knew in college named Mike. He was everything you'd want in a Christian leader—charismatic, talented, the kind of guy who could lead worship, preach a powerful message, and carry a room with ease. Everyone admired Mike. Including his peers in ministry.

But years later, a few trusted friends confronted him. They told him, "You're gifted. You're dynamic. But you're also too blunt. You hurt people with your words. You lack compassion and empathy."

That moment broke him open.

He later said, "I realized not one of the things they praised—my skills, my energy, my intelligence—was a fruit of the Spirit. I found myself praying, *God, I wish I were a little less dynamic and a little more compassionate.*"

Then came the unexpected.

Mike suffered a brain hemorrhage that nearly took his life. It changed everything. He could no longer sing. His appearance shifted. His speech was affected. From the outside, it looked like all the things that made him "successful" in ministry had been stripped away.

But over time, something else began to grow.

Mike eventually helped launch a thriving counseling center. He became a shepherd to fallen pastors, broken marriages, hurting families. His leadership didn't disappear—it deepened. His ministry no longer drew a crowd, but it healed hearts. One at a time.

Gary watched all of this happen and said, "Back then, when I was around Mike, I wanted to be more like Mike. But now—after all he's been through—when I'm around Mike, I want to be more like Jesus."

Fruit had grown in the most unexpected of places.

In the End . . .

If you're still wondering what it all adds up to, Scripture gives us one more glimpse. In Revelation 22, we are given a vision of the garden to come, a restored Eden: "Then the angel showed me the river of the water of life. . . . On each side of the river stood the tree of life, bearing twelve crops of fruit, yielding its fruit every month. And the leaves of the tree are for the healing of the nations. . . . His servants will serve him. . . . And they will reign for ever and ever" (Revelation 22:1–5).

Did you catch that? *Fruit.* Abundant. Eternal. For the healing of the nations.

The cultivated life is not just for now. It is a preview of the garden to come. Every act of love, every seed of joy, every sacrifice of peace, it all echoes into eternity. Every bit of fruit that grows in us here will bloom in full when God's kingdom comes in glory.

And so the question remains: *What will you offer?*

Deuteronomy 26 teaches us to bring our firstfruits before the Lord—not just our crops, but our stories, our identities, our trust.

Proverbs 3:9–10 reminds us: "Honor the Lord with your wealth, with the firstfruits of all your crops; then your barns will be filled to overflowing."

Not because God needs what we produce, but because the act of offering is what reorients our hearts. It's how we say, *You brought me out of slavery. You gave me a future. You are the gardener of my life.*

The cultivated life begins and ends in gratitude.

So give him your first and best.
Offer your fruit.
And remember: It won't always come quickly.
It won't always look impressive.
But it will be real.

Because the Spirit doesn't grow fruit in us overnight. He breaks ground. He tills the soil. He transforms us from the inside out—patiently, persistently, lovingly.

This is not the work of self-help. It is the work of surrender.

And if you're willing to trust the Gardener—if you're willing to let him in, allow him to turn the soil, permit him to plant what only he can grow—then in time, you will find something rooted, something strong, something alive beginning to rise.

You were made for more than warehouse living.
More than surface-level religion.
More than hurry, noise, and striving.

You were made for life in the Spirit.

So here at the end, we return to a new beginning.

Grab a shovel.
Offer your heart.
Let God break the ground.
And watch what he cultivates in you.

NOTES

Preface: How to Get the Most from This Book

- René Schlaepfer also retells this story in his book *Thrill Ride: Thriving Through Life's Ups and Downs* (Twin Lakes Church, 2008).
- "Everything sad will come untrue . . ." This was Timothy Keller paraphrasing Tolkien in various sermons and writings, notably in *Walking with God Through Pain and Suffering* (Viking, 2013).

Introduction: Learning to Tend

- "God loves you just the way you are, but he refuses to leave you that way"—from Max Lucado's *Just like Jesus* (Thomas Nelson, 1998), in chapter 1, "A Heart like His."
- C. S. Lewis, *The Great Divorce* (HarperOne, 1946), chapter 11.

Love: The One Who Won't Let Go

- I saw this ESPN story on Sports Center years ago. My wife says I watch that show too much.

- Josh McDowell and Bob Hostetler, *The New Tolerance: How a Cultural Movement Threatens to Destroy You, Your Faith, and Your Children* (Tyndale, 1998).
- C. S. Lewis, *Mere Christianity* (HarperOne, 1952), chapter 10.

Joy: The One Who Gives You a Song

- David Peterson, former pastor of Memorial Drive Presbyterian Church, tells the story about his daughter's canceled wedding ceremony.

Peace: The One Who Calms the Storm

- For more information and exegesis on Mark chapter 4 and the calming of the storm, see Tim Keller's *Jesus the King: Understanding the Life and Death of the Son of God* (previously titled *King's Cross: The Story of the World in the Life of Jesus*) (Penguin, 2011), chapter 12.
- Mark Buchanan, *Your God Is Too Safe* (Multnomah, 2001), chapter 1.
- Oswald Chambers, *My Utmost for His Highest*, updated ed., ed. James Reimann (Discovery House, 1992), May 29 entry.

Patience: The One Who Waits with You

- James Gleick, *Faster: The Acceleration of Just About Everything* (Pantheon Books, 1999), 176–77.
- Lewis Smedes, *Standing on the Promises* (Thomas Nelson, 1998), 41–42.
- Frederick Marryat (1792–1848) was a British naval officer and one of the early pioneers of nautical fiction. Best known for his adventure novels such as *Mr. Midshipman Easy* and *The Children*

of the New Forest, Marryat drew heavily from his own experience in the Royal Navy during the Napoleonic Wars. His works influenced later writers, such as Joseph Conrad and C. S. Forester, and remain a window into the maritime world of the nineteenth century.

- Max Lucado, *When Christ Comes: The Beginning of the Very Best* (Thomas Nelson, 1999), in the chapter "The Waiting Forwardly" (on Simeon and Anna's story in Luke 2).
- Bruce Feiler's article "A Father's Prayer for His Children" was published in *The New York Times*, June 17, 2011. Feiler is a bestselling author known for *Walking the Bible* and *The Council of Dads*. The essay reflects on lessons learned during his battle with cancer, particularly the spiritual value of slowness, community, and attentiveness.

Kindness: The One Who Pours Out

- John Ortberg recounts the story John Gilbert shared in *Everybody's Normal Till You Get to Know Them* (Zondervan, 2003), in the chapter "Outrageous Sacrifice."
- Dallas Willard, *The Divine Conspiracy: Rediscovering Our Hidden Life in God* (HarperOne, 1998), chapter 1.

Goodness: The One Who Mends What Is Broken

- Robert Coles, "The Disparity Between Intellect and Character," *The Chronicle of Higher Education*, September 22, 1995. The article recounts Coles's conversation with a working-class student at Harvard who challenged the moral integrity of her classmates. She asked, "What's the point of knowing good if you don't keep trying to become a good person?"

Faithfulness: The One Who Keeps His Promises

- Rebecca Allison, "Invisible Jim Earns Company Money for Nothing," *The Guardian*, May 24, 2001. A toy marketed in the UK for roughly £1.99 prided itself on being invisible—literally empty—yet sold out. The packaging featured slogans like "Not seen on TV!" and "Camouflage sold separately," making the toy a cautionary case of marketing over substance.
- The reference on 7,487 promises comes from Max Lucado's *Unshakable Hope: Building Our Lives on the Promises of God* (Thomas Nelson, 2018), chapter 1.
- CNN (March 3, 2023) reports that Japan has officially increased its island count from 6,852 to 14,125 following a new digital survey.
- Vic Pentz is my predecessor at Peachtree Presbyterian Church, and he is one of my ministry heroes.

Gentleness: The One Who Speaks Tenderly

- Researchers Matthias Mehl and colleagues discovered that American adults speak, on average, around sixteen thousand words per day—enough to read the Bible aloud from cover to cover 625 times in a lifetime. They debunked the myth that women use more words than men in "Are Women Really More Talkative Than Men?," *Science* 317, no. 5834 (2007): 822–24.
- Sally Lloyd-Jones and Jago (illustrator), *The Jesus Storybook Bible: Every Story Whispers His Name* (ZonderKidz, 2009). This children's Bible is not just for parents and grandparents.
- Dane C. Ortlund, *Gentle and Lowly: The Heart of Christ for Sinners and Sufferers* (Crossway, 2020), 18.
- Eugene Peterson, *Subversive Spirituality* (Eerdmans, 1997) in the section, "Teach Us to Care and Not to Care."

- Joseph Telushkin, *Words That Hurt, Words That Heal: How to Choose Words Wisely and Well*, rev. ed. (HarperCollins, 2010).

Self-Control: The One Who Trains You

- I've been to Corinth multiple times, and I heard these facts from our local tour guide.
- Charles Duhigg, *The Power of Habit: Why We Do What We Do in Life and Business* (Random House, 2012).
- Giuseppe Berardelli, "Italian Priest Dies of Coronavirus After Giving Up His Ventilator to Help Others," CBS News, March 24, 2020.
- "We don't rise to the level of our expectations . . ." Often attributed to Archilochus, a Greek poet, and popularized by US Navy SEALs and tactical training communities. See James Clear, *Atomic Habits* (Avery, 2018), 163.

Conclusion: The Grand Prize

- I heard Dallas Willard speak this quote in the doctoral class I took with him through Fuller Theological Seminary.
- Karl Barth's parable is shared in Eugene Peterson's *Eat This Book: A Conversation in the Art of Spiritual Reading* (Eerdmans, 2006).
- Gary Thomas, *Authentic Faith* (Zondervan, 2009), 11–13.

ACKNOWLEDGMENTS

Writing a book is never a solo endeavor. And while my name is on the cover, the pages inside bear the fingerprints of so many others. The fruit of the Spirit in them is so evident to me . . .

To my mother—thank you for your patience that gave me room to grow.

To my father—thank you for your gentleness that grounded me.

To Kelly—thank you for your love that sustains me every day.

To Danica—thank you for your faithfulness that deepens me.

To Ashby—thank you for your joy that plays with me.

To the churches I've had the privilege of serving:

To First Presbyterian Church of Houston—thank you for giving me my start.

To Central Presbyterian in Summit, New Jersey—thank you for your patience and trust in my early years.

To First Presbyterian San Antonio—thank you for helping bring me back to faith and showing me what community can look like.

To St. Andrew's Presbyterian in Newport Beach—thank you for being home during some of our most formative years.

And to Peachtree Church in Atlanta—thank you for walking with me in ministry and mission. It's an honor to serve and learn alongside you.

To the families who gave me places to write, reflect, and rest—Aderholds, Borders, Hennesseys, Simms, Sands—thank you for your hospitality and generosity.

To Tom Bell—thank you for pushing me when I needed the nudge to activate.

To Minta Horton—thank you for your sharp eyes and steady support. You made this better than it would have been alone. More commas!

To Morgan Kennedy—I am humbled by your serving spirit and willingness to dig in. You kept this project moving and made me laugh by reading emails to me over the phone that I should have paid attention to. It's almost like you gave birth to this project (see what I did there?) Fewer dashes!

To Mickey Maudlin—thank you for your editorial wisdom and the kindness you brought to every step of the process. I'm grateful for both your skill and your partnership.

And to every person who has read, prayed, encouraged, or believed in one of my sermons—thank you. Your presence reminds me that we don't grow by ourselves.